Sister Renee

Seeds
of
Discord

Seeds
of
Discord

Discerning and Destroying Divisive and Disloyal Spirits

John Tetsola

Bogota, New Jersey

Seeds of Discord
Discerning and Destroying Divisive and Disloyal Spirits

ISBN 1-889389-02-1

Note: In some Scripture quotations, italics have been added by the author for emphasis only.

Table of Contents

INTRODUCTION

The Bible indicates six things that the Lord hates, and a seventh which is an abomination to Him; "he that sows discord among the brethen." The sower of discord is one who plants divisive thoughts that birth separation and division within covenantal relationship. It is interesting to note that Scripture likens one who produces discord to the sower, who literally and figuratively plants seeds. One who plants seeds of discord is actually beginning a crop that will ripen and produce a harvest of devastation within the entire "garden." There are many in the Church of the Lord Jesus Christ who plant these seeds in the minds of believers, causing the brethren to fall away. Seeds of discord will cause individuals to question those that stand in places of authority, and will breed the weeds of rebellion and hatred and destroy the fruit of submission. One becomes a sower of discord when issues of trust are in question, causing resentment, bitterness and hatred. When not properly dealt with, these unresolved issues result in producing divisive, disloyal, and highly dissatisfied individuals who seek out other wounded individuals whom they can poison with their views and disgruntled opinions. These seeds, as is the purpose of seeds to do, will first take root, then grow, and they will flourish into a full blown tree of disloyalty. Then that tree will produce more fruit and more seeds, which will be eaten by and planted in the lives of other individuals. The cycle will continue if the source is not destroyed from the root.

It is even more interesting to note that these people are individuals who may have been wounded due to no fault of their own. Since the Body of Christ has not been made fully aware of the devastation of untreated wounds, healing never comes, and the wounds become infected and fester, producing the fever of resentment, bitterness, and hatred. Offence produces dissatisfaction among the brethren, and ultimately, divisive and disloyal spirits.

We can no longer stand by and allow our wounded soldiers to suffer in the misery of their pain. We must allow the love and compassion of the nature of God to function through us, reach those who are hurting. Many divisive and disloyal people began as sincere wounded sheep whose natures changed when they were wounded. They develop into destructive individuals, and all because no one took the time to walk them through an offence or a breach of trust. It is my prayer that this book will serve as a mirror for those who are hurting, and as a catalyst for those who desire to become healing instruments in the hands of the Master, for we are our brother's keeper!

John Tetsola
October 1996

DEDICATION

This book is dedicated to the eldership, ministers and leaders of Ecclesia Christian Center, honoring their consistent support and endeavors in carrying out their responsibilities towards the people of God and towards the vision of the House without divisiveness or disruption.

CHAPTER I

MARKING THOSE THAT BRING DIVISION

Him that is weak in the faith receive ye, *but* not to doubtful disputations.

For one believeth that he may eat all things: another, who is weak, eateth herbs.

Let not him that eateth despise him that eateth not; and let not him which eateth not judge him that eateth: for God hath received him.

But why dost thou judge thy brother? or why dost thou set at nought thy brother? for we shall all stand before the judgment seat of Christ.

Let us not therefore judge one another any more: but judge this rather, that no man put a stumblingblock or an occasion to fall in *his* brother's way.

But if thy brother be grieved with *thy* meat, now walkest thou not charitably. Destroy not him with thy meat, for whom Christ died.

Let us therefore follow after the things which make for peace, and things wherewith one may edify another.

Romans 14:1-3,10,13,15,19

1

We then that are strong ought to bear the infirmities of the weak, and not to please ourselves.

Let every one of us please *his* neighbor for *his* good to edification.

For even Christ pleased not himself; but, as it is written, The reproaches of them that reproached thee fell on me.

Romans 15:1-3

Paul gave a powerful final message to the Church of Rome, almost out of context from his previous messages in Romans chapters 14 and 15, in which he admonishes us that we have a responsibility to bear the weaknesses of the weak. We are to undergird and bear them like we would lift someone upon our shoulder. We have to have love and patience and care for them. Because Paul's love for the church was Christ's love for the Church, he wanted the church to be strong and healthy. The apparent paradox presents itself in his final message to the Roman Church, when he states that we are to avoid people who bring division into the House of God. We are to mark them and to keep our eyes fastened upon them.

Before this last message, Paul spoke about many things to the Church at Rome. He talked about his ministry, he talked about the people that he loved, and he commended them. Paul's final message of warning was written to a strong church, not a weak and puny assemblage.

The Church at Rome was a strong church. They were not struggling to hang on, but their faith was known throughout the whole world. Yet apparently, they needed this warning. The seriousness of what Paul was teaching must not be lost on today's church, either, for it is the very fabric which will keep the covenantal community of Christ knitted as one Body in the earth.

> Now I beseech you, brethren, mark them which cause divisions and offence contrary to the doctrine which ye have learned; and avoid them.
>
> For they that are such serve not our Lord Jesus Christ, but their own belly; and by good words and fair speeches deceive the hearts of the simple.
>
> For your obedience is come abroad unto all men. I am glad therefore on your behalf: but yet I would have you wise unto that which is good, and simple concerning evil.
>
> And the God of peace shall bruise Satan under your feet shortly. The grace of our Lord Jesus Christ be with you. Amen.
>
> **Romans 16:17-20**

The Bible demands that we mark divisive people and avoid them. In other words, Paul is saying, "Mark what is good and avoid what is evil." This is almost paradoxical because we know that the Word of God admonishes and encourages us to support the weak; that we are to help those that have weaknesses. Some of those weaknesses include being judgmental, critical, legalistic, immature, frustrated and uninformed. These are the character traits of weak people. The Bible encourages we who are strong to bear them, to carry them, to support them, to be patient with them and to love them. The Bible repeats this command in the 14th chapter of the book of Romans.

Now, all of a sudden, Paul seems to be singing a different tune. Yet his instructions do not contradict the commandment to bear the infirmities of the weak. Paul appears to place the weak in one category and divisive people in another. Paul understood that there were certain tactics used by the enemy that were initiated to ruin the work of God. Divisiveness and evil are a threat to the Church. The Church will always be the Church, but it can be destroyed from within. If Satan can get into the Church and begin to sow his seeds within the hearts of believers, then his ideologies become a threat to the integrity of the Church. Paul knew this fact.

You and I live in a corrupt world. We live in the midst of contamination all week long. Every society outside of the Church is polluted and ravaged by the presence of sin. We live in a world that is called a "rat race." It is a world in which everybody is out to get ahead, no matter what it takes and who it hurts. We live in that type of atmosphere. The general mentality is "get ahead, climb up the ladder of success no matter what it costs you." Ambition is untamed, so there is tremendous tension that manifests in every facet of life. Manipulation and politics are standard tools of operation. We live in that kind of climate. When we come into the House of God, we must rid ourselves of all that contamination. That is one reason why our church utilizes a prayer room. We walk in there before we even sit down to listen to the Lord. We go before the Lord, and we wash ourselves well. We cleanse our minds and our thoughts of all that perverts the Word of God. We pray in the Spirit and worship the Lord, so that when we come into the service or start to relate and fellowship with our fellow Christians, we can lift up clean hands and a pure heart.

When we go out to the world, we come up against the same thing that Satan would like to put in the Church— people that are disgruntled, disappointed, unhappy, offended and selfish. It is important to realize that if we are not careful, we are subject to those same attitudes. It is easy to assume the

4

wrong attitudes, for we can be offended very easily. It is even easier for us to become the offender. We must stay on our guard so that we don't become a habitation for these spirits. We must make sure that we allow the Spirit of God in us to continually have His way in us. We must confess the problems and the offenses that intrude into our lives, and admit that we may be at fault. Don't be surprised when someone who is a strong believer becomes disgruntled, upset or divisive. It happens, so don't ever be surprised. Just exercise wisdom so that you can minister to them, instead of taking up their offense.

STAY AWAY FROM THE ACCUSER!

There are three reasons why a divisive person must be marked and avoided. You see, a divisive person is a person who lays a stumblingblock in front of another person and causes their growth either to stop or become stagnated. The purpose of the enemy is to stop the spiritual development of an individual. I know that as a pastor, there are times people get upset with me. The sad thing is not the fact that they get upset, but that they begin to react from their anger, rather than respond in wisdom. I have watched people whom I have been feeding well, who were once taking notes, listening and following the Scriptures, all of a sudden become disgruntled because of an offense that they have picked up. Their attendance becomes erratic, they stop serving, they pout, and their attitude keeps them from receiving the Word of God. They can no longer hear my voice. Some of them just stop eating entirely.

What happens in the natural when you stop eating? Physically, you get weaker and weaker, and you become more susceptible to disease. Your whole system gets run down because there is no nourishment. Suddenly you are picking up germs that you would have been able to resist easily. You will pick up infections that normally would not have been able to touch you.

This same principle works when you get caught in an offense. You literally refuse to eat when you are nurturing an offense. You can sit in church for years and hear messages, but because of bitterness toward the membership, leadership, or eldership, you simply stop eating. Although outwardly you may look like you are still with it, you are going down, down, down and out. You are a prime target for all the diseases of sin, further offenses, criticism, divisiveness and manipulation to come into your life. These things would eventually destroy you. These things must be watched very carefully. Divisiveness and offenses must be handled in the Biblical way.

The word "division" means "standing apart from the whole." It means "to be separated or cause cleavage." Once you used to be in the whole, but division came and now you are not part of the whole. You are separated from the whole. "Offense" is defined as "laying a stumblingblock," or "causing people to fall." When offenses come, they cause people to fall. The Bible says that these are the reasons that we are to avoid divisive and easily offended people, who separate themselves from the whole, thereby creating a stumblingblock that causes others to fall.

FOUR INGREDIENTS OF A GENUINE BELIEVER

(a)   A genuine believer trusts God. Sometimes we have to shake ourselves in the midst of our trouble and tribulations. A genuine believer trusts God no matter what.

(b)   A genuine believer makes Jesus Christ Lord. He is Lord of their families, businesses, jobs and finances.

(c)   Genuine Christians love one another. This is the evidence Jesus spoke of when He said you have "passed from death unto life." This is how you know that you are a Christian, because you love one another.

(d)   A genuine believer desires to see the gospel of Jesus Christ spread throughout the whole world, starting with his neighborhood, his city and his state.

Now when division and offenses come, guess what happens to those priorities? Suddenly, the individual opposes the authority of Jesus in his life because of disobedience. He is stuck in the morass of unforgiveness. He only tolerates his brother. So, the throne of that individual's heart is no longer occupied by the Lordship of Jesus Christ, but instead, he has become lord. It is now all about "I." He tells himself "I have been hurt. I have been offended and they have no right to do that to me. I will get even with them." These thoughts diminish the Lordship of Christ.

When a person starts thinking like this, they smother the natural impulse to love people. At one time, they were very loving. They would come in the midst of the congregation and declare their love for others. Now they come into the midst of the congregation and become critical of the House of God. The House of God is not a building. The House of God is constructed of the children of God. It is you and I. When you have an offense against the Church, it is not against the building but against the people, starting with the senior leader of the house down to the eldership team and so on. The moment you pick up those offenses, Satan is using the tool of division to get you to separate yourself and pull away so you no longer value things from the whole. He causes you to focus on your part. All of a sudden you begin to find fault in everything that is said and done.

You lose your vision. This is an amazing thing, because once you become divisive, you have one thing in mind. You want the Church hurt just because you have been hurt by somebody. You desire to see the Church fail, and will try to justify your own bad feelings. You want to see the vision of the Church completely collapse, and your hardened demands to be right. The danger is that you have become deaf, and you can no longer hear the Truth; you reject any other perspective, except that which is formed by your own defensive heart.

WARNING! WARNING! WARNING! WARNING!

I urge you, brothers, to watch out for those who cause divisions and put obstacles in your way that are contrary to the teaching you have learned. Keep away from them.

For such people are not serving our Lord Christ, but their own appetites. By smooth talk and flattery they deceive the minds of naive people.

Romans 16:17-18 (NIV)

Paul begins to declare an urgent message to the Roman Church. He says, "I urge brethren (male and female

8

alike) to mark the individuals that cause division and offenses in the midst of the church." This word "mark" does not denote a negative action, as is many times perceived. To "mark" does not mean to mistreat or take revenge on someone. Paul was not preaching to let go of our Christ-like attributes and stoop to the level of those causing division and offense.

Instead, when Paul warns us to "mark" these individuals, he is using the Greek word "skopeo," which means "to scope, consider, spy, scout or to observe." In other words, Paul's advice is to "scope out these individuals." Consider and scout out the people who are in our midst, sowing seeds of discord. Observe those who are laying obstacles in your way or the way of your fellow believers. Consider and scope out those who are constantly pulling you in a direction opposite and contrary to the teachings that you have learned.

The word "mark" also means "to keep one's eye upon, to observe, to focus, and to scrutinize." In other words, don't let them get out of your sight because that person is a serious threat to the church. So you must watch them carefully. You make sure that you avoid them and that you are not involved with them.

Paul then goes on further to say that you then must stay clear of these people. In other words, "Avoid them!!" The word "avoid" means "to shun." It means "to turn away, to keep away, to remove oneself, and to have nothing to do with another." If a person is divisive, the Bible tells us that we are to turn away, to remove ourselves, and keep away from people who are divisive and who bring offenses to the Body. The enemy desires to get people to stumble just like the person carrying the offense has stumbled. The enemy wants you to stumble with them so that you can agree with them and be separated from the whole.

MARK AND AVOID DIVISIVE PEOPLE

It is important to understand this. First, if you don't avoid them, you will lend your approval to their actions by your company and identification with them. You are sending the signal to everyone else that they are all right, that they can bring division, that they can pull people away from the House of God, and that you are just being a friend.

Second, you risk stumbling yourself. I don't care who you are (and I have watched this repeatedly over the years), but when someone has picked up a serious offense against the house of God, they become bitter and resentful. They'll decide to leave the House of God and then someone says, "I am going to try to bring them back," or "I am just going to spend time with them," and they become friends. When such individuals are told to be careful with the divisive person, they'll invariably say, "Oh! No problem! I am preaching to him all the time. They have a bad attitude and I know that they have to change." It may take some people a short time and it may take some people a longer time, but if they keep that friendship close and intact, to the point where they are running together, being buddies and having fun with the person who has bitterness and an offense against the house of God, sooner or later, because that individual is violating Scripture, he will pick up the same offense. Sooner or later they are going to be history themselves-- out of the house of God. The seeds of division are highly contagious. Paul prescribes marking and separation because you risk picking up the same thing.

In reality, many Christians fluctuate. Some days they're up and some days they're down. Some days they feel great and some days they don't even feel like a Christian. Some days everything pleases them, and some days nothing pleases them. Now, imagine if you are in one of your "down days;" if you keep company with a person who is divisive, what do you think is going to happen to you? You are going to end up assimilating the stench of their offense. You'll start smelling just like them.

Third, God's disciplinary action demands separation. There is only one discipline that you can put on a brother or sister who is taken with a fault, who won't repent and who continues in that fault. There is only one Biblical discipline and that is to withdraw fellowship. You must be able to look them in the face and say, "I am sorry sister. I am not willing to allow what you have in your spirit to poison my spirit. If you change your attitude, we can be friends. But as long as you still have that attitude, we can't hang together anymore."

TO SERVE CHRIST NO MORE

For they that are such serve not our Lord Jesus Christ, but their own belly; and by good words and fair speeches deceive the hearts of the simple.

Romans 16:18

A divisive person does not serve the Lord. This is very important to understand. I don't care if they have a Christian title, a divisive person does not serve the Lord. How do you serve the Lord? There is only one way that you can serve the Lord. You cannot climb out of this world, climb onto a cloud or up to the sky and serve Jesus somewhere. You serve Jesus right here in this body. This is the expression of Jesus upon the earth in which He is vitally interested. He has a body that expresses His personality. If you say, "I like the Spirit of Jesus, but I don't like His body," that would be like walking up to me and saying, "Brother John, I think you are a nice person" and then you slap me in the face. Then when I ask why you did that, you say that you like me but you cannot stand my body. Wait a minute! You cannot separate me from my body. Jesus said the same thing in Ephesians 5; "the two are one flesh." The Church is His body.

If you are serving Jesus Christ, you cannot be divisive and cut the body to pieces. You cannot separate your part from the whole and say, "I am serving Jesus Christ." No, you are not serving the Lord! You are serving your belly. In the old King James days, that was okay. What it simply meant was that you were serving yourself. You want your own way. You want to fulfill your own selfish desires, your personal urges, your physical appetite. You are living your own self-centered life. You are not serving the Lord, because if you serve the Lord you will always think of the whole, even if you are in trouble personally.

Everyone of us gets in trouble personally. Everyone of us has times when we are hurt, injured, disappointed and weak. That is okay. What brings us to maturity is that even though we disagree and at times want our way, we are more conscious of the Body than of our own personal agenda. We are willing to let go our agenda in order to connect with the main agenda of the Body. Divisive people— people who want to take a piece of the Body unto themselves— are not serving the Lord Jesus. They are serving their own bellies and they are enemies of the Cross. They are not committed to His honor and His glory. They lose the vision of the whole because of their offenses.

For many walk, of whom I have told you often, and now tell you even weeping, that they are the enemies of the cross of Christ:

Whose end is destruction, whose God is their belly, and whose glory is in their shame, who mind earthly things.

Philippians 3:18,19

Paul began to inform the church at Philippi that there were individuals that became "enemies" of the cross of Christ. In other words, there were those that were perverting the Gospel of Christ (Galatians 1:7) and walked contrary to the Word of God. A reason for this disruptive walk was that their god was actually their "belly." Paul was not speaking of a literal belly or abdomen, but he was speaking figuratively of the heart. He was saying that people who cause division flow as such because their god is their own appetite. Their god is their own fleshly desires. The desires of the cross no longer appealed to them. Their own agendas reigned supreme. Paul notifies the church that the destination of these individuals always ends in an arena of destruction.

FLATTERY IS A TRAP

For they that are such serve not our Lord Jesus Christ, but their own belly; and by good words and fair speeches deceive the hearts of the simple.

Romans 16:18

Divisive people use flattering words and they deceive the simple. The use of the word "simple" here does not mean "an ignorant or retarded person." It means a person who is pure, undefiled and very open. Divisive people can deceive that person because he believes in them and believes in people. He trusts people. He believes they won't hurt him. Absalom, David's son, inflicted this same tactic on the people of David's kingdom for forty solid years and reaped devastating results. (We will go further into this in the next chapter). God loves His Church and when someone is divisive, you don't have to fight your own battle. You don't have to defend yourself. God will fight your battle! He will stand against the divisive thing that is taking place in the House of God! Don't ever be afraid of divisive people, because God will always take care of them.

CHAPTER II

THE DEVASTATION OF DISLOYALTY

And it came to pass after this, that Absalom prepared him chariots and horses, and fifty men to run before him.

And Absalom rose up early, and stood beside the way of the gate: and it was so, that when any man that had a controversy came to the king for judgment, then Absalom called unto him, and said, Of what city art thou? And he said, Thy servant is of one of the tribes of Israel.

And Absalom said unto him, See, thy matters are good and right; but there is no man deputed of the king to hear thee.

Absalom said moreover, Oh that I were made judge in the land, that every man which hath any suit or cause might come unto me, and I would do him justice!

And it was so, that when any man came nigh to him to do him obeisance, he put forth his hand, and took him, and kissed him.

And on this manner did Absalom to all Israel that came to the king for judgment: so Absalom stole the hearts of the men of Israel.

II Samuel 15:1-6

In the Scripture, the name of Absalom is forever tainted with the memory of evil. Absalom developed a reputation for being cruel, disloyal, and unwise. He devastated not only his life, but he caused the deaths of twenty thousand of the choice men of Israel and brought untold agony to his family. He died in the end because of the beauty of his head.

Absalom was a unique young man. He was gifted with remarkable beauty, commanding presence, natural dignity, and extraordinary grace, charm and eloquence. Yet a treacherous nature lurked within him. Absalom had unresolved offenses which led him to hate, sow seeds of discord and to betray David, his own father. His ego, pride and selfishness led him to believe he could have anything he wanted, and that he was a better leader than the great King David. His disloyalty led him to devise a murderous plot toward his family. He was willing to attack David so that his own egotistical spirit could be satisfied.

> **But Absalom sent spies throughout all the tribes of Israel, saying, As soon as ye hear the sound of the trumpet, then ye shall say, Absalom reigneth in Hebron.**
>
> **And with Absalom went two hundred men out of Jerusalem, *that were* called; and they went in their simplicity, and they knew not any thing.**
>
> **II Samuel 15:10,11**

You will always risk gathering men and women who will exploit the local church for their own purposes and will not care for the flock, as a true shepherd would. The men and women we all want have an unoffended, uncomplaining heart that trusts God's ways, His unexplained dealings with the soul, and His ordering of life. These kinds of men and women are rare, but they can be found.

It is Satan's strategy to bring down leadership and to bring down churches. Absalom used legitimate and innocent complaints to steal the hearts of the people. His motive was not to resolve an offense; but his motive was to create followers. They came for justice, but before they had a chance to go through the process, he planted a seed in their minds that they were not going to get justice. Absalom was bitter towards his father, and sought to exonerate himself in his own conscience that he would be a better king than his father.

When Absalom's half-brother committed immorality, Absalom was angry. He wanted his father to chasten his half-brother and David did not do it. Absalom became bitter toward David. He nurtured his offense. This offense caused him to respond in a negative way. He said, "I don't think that David is running things right around here, because David should have disciplined my brother and he did not do it." Bitterness became Absalom's motivation. Often divisive people have unresolved offenses or conflicts. Someone made a decision with which they did not agree. They never tried to resolve it the way the Bible recommends. Instead, they have become divisive by tearing away from the whole and forgetting that they are part of the Body.

Absalom also had a terrible fear that he would not be remembered. He had a terrible fear about his own reputation, so he set out to build himself a kingdom. He set out to build himself a place in his father's house. He plotted for forty years to kill his father. He talked about it in his sleep; and he dreamed about it. He planned it out. He was so consumed with it that when men would come to the kingdom to see his father, every day he would step out from behind the gate and say, "Excuse me. Where are you from?" and they would say, "I am from the tribe of Dan." He would ask them what the problem was, they would tell him the problem and he would say, "Well, I can solve it," and truly the problem was solved. But before they left he would always drop a word in their ears saying "If I were king, things would have been different and you would not be going through what you are presently experiencing...." Absalom did that for over forty years. He undermined the authority of his father, and divided the loyalties of the people. One by one, Absalom patiently stole the heart of the people. David was unaware of the evil that was lurking in his son because he trusted Absalom. David had a good heart toward Absalom. He loved Absalom more than any other son he had.

THE BLINDNESS OF LOVE

And the king commanded Joab and Abishai and Ittai, saying, *Deal* gently for my sake with the young man, *even* with Absalom. And all the people heard when the king gave all the captains charge concerning Absalom.

And the king said unto Cushi, Is the young man Absalom safe? And Cushi answered, The enemies of my lord the king, and all that rise against thee to do *thee* hurt, be as *that* young man *is*.

And the king was much moved, and went up to the chamber over the gate, and wept: and as he went, thus he said, O my son Absalom, my son, my son Absalom! would God I had died for thee, O Absalom, my son, my son!

II Samuel 18:5,32-33

And it was told Joab, Behold, the king weepeth and mourneth for Absalom.

And Joab came into the house to the king, and said, Thou hast shamed this day the faces of all thy servants, which this day have saved thy life, and the lives of thy sons and of thy daughters, and the lives of thy wives, and the lives of thy concubines;

In that thou lovest thine enemies, and hatest thy friends. For thou hast declared this day, that thou regardest neither princes nor servants: for this day I perceive, that if Absalom had lived, and all we had died this day, then it had pleased thee well.

Now therefore arise, go forth, and speak comfortably unto thy servants: for I swear by the LORD, if thou go not forth, there will not tarry one with thee this night: and that will be worse unto thee than all the evil that befell thee from thy youth until now.

Then the king arose, and sat in the gate. And they told unto all the people, saying, Behold, the king doth sit in the gate. And all the people came before the king: for Israel had fled every man to his tent.

II Samuel 19:1,5-8

Love and trust is often blind. Sometimes relationships blind us to other people's weaknesses. David was blinded. If somebody had come to David at the early stages of Absalom's plot, he probably would not have believed it. Why? Because he loved and cared for Absalom. Absalom, realizing the depth of trust, love and confidence that his father had for him, used it as a platform to split his father's kingdom. David was blind concerning the plot of his son, even up to the time of Absalom's death. David could not accept the truth about his son. He was in a complete state of denial. Even after he was told of the uprising and the death of Absalom, David grieved over him so much that Joab told David if he did not shape up, go out and tell his army that he was thankful that they saved the kingdom, that what had happened to him up to this point would be nothing compared to what was going to happen to him.

David came to his senses and went forward to meet his armies. They were afraid of David. An Absalom spirit is a terrible thing. It can destroy our churches, our relationships and can affect everything we do. I, for one, do not want to walk with Absaloms. I don't want them by my side. I don't want them guarding my back. I don't want them to my right or left. I don't want them in front of me. It might take years for an Absalom to surface, because a pure Absalom is a man that is well-gifted in his deceit. He is not a man who stumbles around in error when it comes to laying the net of disloyalty. He is a man who is shrewd; a man who knows how to lay the net. Absaloms are dangerous people. They are dangerous to the Church and they are very dangerous to leadership. They are dangerous in marriages and they are dangerous on the job.

THE SPIRIT OF ABSALOM

There are many Absalom spirits thriving in the twentieth century today. I want you to know that the spirit that really annoys the Absalom mentality is the spirit of the devil. Lucifer was the first Absalom. Lucifer was the first disloyal angel. He was the first living being that crossed God and tried to steal the hearts of the angels to worship him instead of God. Lucifer's spirit still prevails in minds and hearts today. We need not be so naive as to think that we would be above the Absalom spirit. No one reading this book is above the Absalom spirit. We are all carnal men; made of clay. We all have our weaknesses and we all have a thing called "a naughty heart." Jeremiah said the heart is so wicked that no one knows it. Your heart and my heart, even though we are cleansed by the blood of Jesus and we are new creatures in Christ, still deals with a sly carnal man who knows how to manipulate others to get his way. We deal with an ego that is far too large and a carnal mind that is far too smart. And if you ever think that you are above the Absalom spirit, you are already snared and you are probably operating under that spirit already. You will be manipulated and deceived by your own heart.

UNDERSTANDING LOYALTY

For a man to trust his heart, he must be a fool. You must trust God and not your heart because out of your heart, like the Bible says, come lies, murder and all evil things. Absalom is a shining example of something we don't want to become. Let's just understand what he is to make sure we are not like him. First, let's discuss the definition of loyalty. Out of that, we will be able to get a clear understanding of disloyalty.

Loyalty means "to be faithful; to be constant and true in any relationship; not undermining authority by your words, actions or attitude." We live in a generation that undermines authority continually with word, action and attitude. The resistance of authority has become an acceptable alternative in this society. Even the Church has stooped to tolerating gossiping, murmuring, backbiting, and the questioning of authority.

But if we are going to be people of the Word of God, then we will nurture the qualities that will build integrity in our lives. Loyalty means "to stand with those you are serving in their time of need." Loyalty is being a reliable messenger to those you are serving -- being a mirror and a reflector of truth to those you are serving. Loyalty cannot be tested unless there are problems and fire. Nobody knows if they are loyal until they get into a battle and stand with the person to whom they say they are loyal. Love is not tested when you love each other. Love is tested when you have a fight. Loyalty is not tested when everything is going well. Loyalty is tested when everything is not going well. When David was not out there taking care of the affairs of the city, maybe David was busy taking care of the strategic aspect of the kingdom. Maybe he was busy sitting back on his laurels, enjoying forty years of activity. I don't know where David was or what he was doing before Absalom divided his kingdom, but the fact to understand is that wherever he was, it was all right. Absalom had no right to question what David was doing or to undermine his leadership in the kingdom. Absalom was totally wrong, but he created his evil slowly and strategically. Loyalty is constant and firm in relationships. It is standing with those you love in the time of their storms and in the time of their wars.

Loyalty is learning when to "zip it up." It is learning when to close your mouth and ears. Loyalty is standing with someone when they are under fire— when the enemy is shooting away, when you have questions about them, when you are not sure, and the Lord says, "Stand with them," and you say, "I don't understand, but yes, Lord." Loyalty is staying on the team when you are sitting on the bench. It is not yelling at the coach when the crowd gets upset over the wrong play, even when you know that it was the wrong play or the wrong call. Loyalty is standing with the coach when the public won't. It is a state of the heart and not an emotion. It is what we are in our character and not just in our mind.

THE DISLOYAL PERSON

After looking at what a loyal person is, let's look at some of the characteristics of a disloyal person.

A disloyal person is very likable. Absalom was a very likable person. He had beautiful hair and was very good looking. He was the kind of guy you would like to be around. If you were choosing up teams, you would have chosen Absalom. If you were going out for coffee, you would want him with you. If you saw him in a football game, you would go sit with him. He was just a flat-out likable guy. But what you saw is not what you got. He was likable because of his charisma, and charisma can be quite manipulative. If the person lacks character, the power of their charisma can become quite damaging.

THE SPIRIT OF SHREWDNESS

And Absalom said unto him, See, thy matters *are* good and right; but *there is* no man *deputed* of the king to hear thee.

Absalom said moreover, Oh that I were made judge in the land, that every man which hath any suit or cause might come unto me, and I would do him justice!

II Samuel 15:3-4

A disloyal person is very shrewd. Absalom was very shrewd. His disloyalty was planned. His disloyalty was mapped out. His words were chosen. His timing was exact. He knew what he was doing. He didn't speak an accidental negative word. As a leader, I have found that usually, the actions of disloyal people were not so accidental. They planned, worked, moved and positioned themselves in order to make things happen.

Disloyal people normally have a planned strategy. Absalom had a planned strategy. Not only was he shrewd, he stole the hearts of the people one by one. He had patience for forty years. He worked for it. He was a man of determination and that determination was an ungodly drive. He was a driven man; he was patient, but there is such a thing as exercising ungodly determination and patience to get what you want. There is that disloyal patience and that disloyal determination that God looks on and rules as ungodly.

NEGATIVE INFLUENCES

And Absalom sent for Ahithophel the Gilonite, David's counsellor, from his city, *even* from Giloh, while he offered sacrifices. And the conspiracy was strong; for the people increased continually with Absalom.

And *one* told David, saying, Ahithophel *is* among the conspirators with Absalom. And David said, O LORD, I pray thee, turn the counsel of Ahithophel into foolishness.

II Samuel 15:12,31

And the counsel of Ahithophel, which he counselled in those days, *was* as if a man had inquired at the oracle of God: so *was* all the counsel of Ahithophel both with David and with Absalom.

II Samuel 16:23

Disloyal people always exert a negative influence. Absalom was a negative influence. He won over key leaders of David to his side. He lured David's chief counselor, who today would be similar to the prime minister of a nation. He won over Ahithophel, who stood as David's advisor and counselor.

Absalom slowly wooed Ahithophel into his plan. How? He spent time stroking the mixed motives within the heart of Ahithophel. He stroked his ambition and fed his ego by telling him, "Ahithophel, you know, if I were in Dad's place, I'd pay you more. Your counsel is so good that it is better than the Book of Proverbs." He flattered Ahithophel. He told him all the things his ears longed to hear. "You are the greatest! You are the wisest! You are the best!" He seduced Ahithophel, and caused him to believe that David had been undermining him. He beguiled Ahithophel by promising him that if he jumped camp, he would be compensated more for his worth, gifts and ability than he ever had. Ahithophel did not know what Absalom was doing. His problem was that he had a heart to respond to it. There was something already defective in his heart that made it very easy for him to respond to it. He probably felt unappreciated by David, or was nurturing an offense of his own. He had an ear to hear the enchantments of Absalom.

Finally, when the time was right, Absalom approached Ahithophel and let him know he was going to overthrow his father. He then asked Ahithophel if he were willing to change camp. Ahithophel was not the least bit hesitant. When Ahithophel gave a positive response and agreed to join Absalom, he signed a death warrant on his own life because God heard him.

The secret problem with disloyalty is that it is never between you and a person. You're not fighting with your pastor or eldership. You're not fighting your leaders. The real battle is between you and God. God hates disloyalty. You can never hide it from His eyes. You can never shove it under a carpet somewhere. You can never swallow your words back. God hears when you speak; when you are off in a corner ripping and tearing someone apart. You think only your good, disloyal buddy heard it, but you are wrong. God heard you. God heard what Ahithophel did, and God turned the counsel that Ahithophel gave Absalom into foolishness. David did not do it. God did it. If you think that you can operate a divisive spirit in a church or in ministry without God knowing, you'd better wise up and know that He hears, and God will execute any judgment that is necessary.

God has a real problem with disloyalty. God does not like it. God cannot stand aside and allow a divisive person to split His Church. God will intervene, so if you sense in yourself a divisive spirit for your church or ministry, you'd better stop it right now. It will cost you a lot. It might even cost you your destiny.

MANIPULATIVE CHARISMA

Another characteristic of a disloyal person is manipulative charisma. He used his gift to get his way. Charisma is a gifting and it is a dangerous thing. You can use your charisma to get your way or to do God's will. Absalom had a terrific gift. He was able to use it to steal people's hearts. The definition of leadership in actuality is influence. It is simply the ability to move people's hearts. When God calls you to leadership, to function in the Body, you have the ability to move people's hearts. Think about it-- the counseling, praying, caring, singing, etc. People are moved. Your gift is dangerous. That is why it must be wrapped up with strong character and integrity. We are all dangerous unless God helps us.

WRONG AMBITION

The next characteristic of disloyalty is what I call wrong ambition. Absalom had wrong ambition. He wanted to make a name for himself. He wanted a pillar that would have his name inscribed on it. From the very beginning, he had an ungodly ambition to push himself to the place where he could have reputation, recognition and honor. He had a drive in him for position and not for service. He wanted the glory without the suffering. It is like being a parent but not wanting your children in your home until they are married and have good children. You don't want to change their diapers, discipline them, feed them or pay for their schooling. You don't want the responsibility, but you want the benefit of parenthood. That was Absalom's ambition. He did not want the suffering. He did not want to do what David did. He did not want the wars. All he wanted was a kingdom for himself and he was determined to get it. But God would not allow it because it was a contradiction of how He makes leaders. Absalom was determined to make himself a king and he died for his ambition.

PRIDE IS A KILLER

Absalom's pride and his gift killed him. It was not the oak tree that hung him. It was his pride that hung him. His own great gifts finally killed him because he was not willing to mix the gift with the proper character that is only imparted by God Himself. Look at what the Scripture says: "A man's gift shall make room for him and will bring him before great men." Know this, child of God; your gift will make room for you and will bring you before kings, but your gift will not keep you before kings. God is not just concerned about your coming before kings. He is much more concerned about your staying with kings. God is concerned about the "keeping" part. The "keeping" part can only come into existence where there is the instilling of character. The gift brings you— but your character keeps you before the king. That is why it is not surprising to see great men and women of God who possess great gifting, that were once thrust before great audiences and before great men. They once received great notoriety and popularity, yet find themselves and their ministries in disgrace, shame and sin. When you place great emphasis on your gifts, you will pay dearly. A strong and excellent ministry is only produced when there is a mixture of strong gifts with strong character. Your gifting must be wrapped in an excellent character.

THE STRENGTH OF DISLOYALTY

Now Korah, the son of Izhar, the son of Kohath, the son of Levi, and Dathan and Abiram, the sons of Eliab, and On, the son of Peleth, sons of Reuben, took men:

And they rose up before Moses, with certain of the children of Israel, two hundred and fifty princes of the assembly, famous in the congregation, men of renown:

And they gathered themselves together against Moses and against Aaron, and said unto them, *Ye take* too much upon you, seeing all the congregation *are* holy, every one of them, and the LORD *is* among them: wherefore then lift ye up yourselves above the congregation of the LORD?

And Moses said, Hereby ye shall know that the LORD hath sent me to do all these works; for *I have* not *done them* of mine own mind.

If these men die the common death of all men, or if they be visited after the visitation of all men; *then* the LORD hath not sent me.

But if the LORD make a new thing, and the earth open her mouth, and swallow them up, with all that *appertain* unto them, and they go down quick into the pit; then ye shall understand that these men have provoked the LORD.

And it came to pass, as he had made an end of speaking all these words, that the ground clave asunder that *was* under them:

And the earth opened her mouth, and swallowed them up, and their houses, and all the men that *appertained* unto Korah, and all *their* goods.

They, and all that *appertained* to them, went down alive into the pit, and the earth closed upon them: and they perished from among the congregation.

And all Israel that *were* round about them fled at the cry of them: for they said, Lest the earth swallow us up *also*.

And there came out a fire from the LORD, and consumed the two hundred and fifty men that offered incense.

Numbers 16:1-3, 28-35

Notice that of the two people who were going to rise, one of them is of the genealogy of the priesthood and the other is of the genealogy of Reuben, who was the firstborn and who had the right to the double portion. The Reubenites were the firstborn and possessed the right to the double portion. You can see that these men were not just menial, inexperienced men. They were men who understood God. These were two wonderful tribes that shared a great heritage. Notice their influences. They started with three and they quickly rose to two hundred and fifty men. The spirit of disloyalty spreads very quickly when it is not tamed and killed straight from its root. These were two hundred and fifty of the elders, the choice prophets, evangelists, pastors, teachers and apostles. These were the best of the flocks. You could not ask for anyone better than these men. Korah, Dathan and Abiram were able to influence these men.

Child of God, I want you to know that the spirit of Absalom has great influence from the least to the greatest. Don't be deceived! This divisive spirit can influence anyone, if they are not properly planted. Because of this divisive spirit, God allowed fire to come down and consume the two hundred and fifty men. God honored Moses, not because Moses was blameless or faultless, because Moses had sin in his life. Moses definitely had sin, because God said to him one day, right before they went into the promised land, which Moses had given his life to lead the people into, "Moses, hold it. You are not going in." Moses said, "What do you mean I'm not going in? For eighty years I have waited for this day." God said, "No, Moses. You are not going in. Remember when I told you to smite the rock once and you hit it three times because you were angry? I told you that day that your sin was upon you. Today, Moses, I am collecting. You are not going in. You never controlled that spirit of anger. You did not do what I asked you to do." Moses had problems.

Leadership will always have sin. If you are looking for a sinless leader, you are looking the wrong way. We are all sinners, saved by grace. If you are looking for someone who will never make mistakes, you are looking the wrong way. If you are looking for someone to worship and put on a pedestal, or some kind of a leadership guru, you are looking the wrong way. If you are looking for someone to lead you, to tell you the truth, preach to you the Bible and do his best, then you are looking the right way. Otherwise, you are setting yourself up in a bad place to entertain a divisive spirit. Like Korah, Dathan and Abiram, you will say, "You take too much upon you." You must understand that Moses did not take anything upon him. It was given to him by God. This is the difference. Moses was exactly what they said, "Above the congregation and above them." But he did not take his elevation. It was given. No leader can take authority. If God does not honor it, no one can take it. I cannot say to people, "You follow me." God has to put that in people's hearts. But if God honors the man and God places a pastor, a deacon, an elder or a leader in his office, child of God, please do not speak against God's leaders. It is God that sets the man, the elder, the deacon or the leader in that position.

If we don't respect the leaders that God gives us, then we will never eat the good fruit of our land. It is a spiritual law. It is a principle. God honors authority. When He gives it, He stands solidly behind it. Even when the man is not perfect, God still stands with the man. I am not saying that man can get away with ungodly things without God judging him. God will judge an ungodly leader. I think God judges and deals with any minister or any leader who goes off the track. It may seem like God is not doing anything, but sooner or later God will deal with them. If we try to deal with them, we will end up dealing with our own lives.

And the men of David said unto him, Behold the day of which the LORD said unto thee, Behold, I will deliver thine enemy into thine hand, that thou mayest do to him as it shall seem good unto thee. Then David arose, and cut off the skirt of Saul's robe privily.

And it came to pass afterward, that David's heart smote him, because he had cut off Saul's skirt.

31

And he said unto his men, The LORD forbid that I should do this thing unto my master, the LORD'S anointed, to stretch forth mine hand against him, seeing he *is* the anointed of the LORD.

So David stayed his servants with these words, and suffered them not to rise against Saul. But Saul rose up out of the cave, and went on *his* way.

I Samuel 24:4-7

So David and Abishai came to the people by night: and, behold, Saul lay sleeping within the trench, and his spear stuck in the ground at his bolster: but Abner and the people lay round about him.

Then said Abishai to David, God hath delivered thine enemy into thine hand this day: now therefore let me smite him, I pray thee, with the spear even to the earth at once, and I will not *smite* him the second time.

And David said to Abishai, Destroy him not: for who can stretch forth his hand against the LORD'S anointed, and be guiltless?

David said furthermore, *As* the LORD liveth, the LORD shall smite him; or his day shall come to die; or he shall descend into battle, and perish.

The LORD forbid that I should stretch forth mine hand against the LORD'S anointed: but, I pray thee, take thou now the spear that *is* at his bolster, and the cruse of water, and let us go.

I Samuel 26:7-11

When David was in the cave and Saul came in to take a little nap, his men said, "David, now! Now!" And David said, "Now what?" They said, "David, draw your sword and kill Saul. Can't you see that God has given Saul into your hand to kill him? Your running days are over. Kill him!

32

Don't let him go. He is an old pervert. Kill him!" David said, "I will not touch the Lord's anointed." You can almost see the expression on their faces. They might have been thinking, "Well, he's not the Lord's anointed, you are," but David understood that as long as Saul is king, he is the Lord's anointed. David recognized the chain of command. God put Saul in, so let God take Saul out. And God did. That is why David would never have that guilt on his hands. Even after Saul's death, David cried and mourned. Why was he mourning and crying? Because he is saying this, "God, don't let me be a Saul." He was not just mourning over Saul. He was mourning over what the authority, blessing and honor had done to Saul. He was crying, "Oh God! I am king now. What happened to him could possibly happen to me." You see, authority and blessing are dangerous things. They can turn a man's heart. That is why God is so picky about our personal lives. He's not stingy with power, authority, or blessings. On the contrary, He knows that if He gives a better blessing to the wrong person at the wrong time, it is like cutting their spiritual throat.

> **Wherefore the rather, brethren, give diligence to make your calling and election sure: for if ye do these things, ye shall never fall:**
>
> **II Peter 1:10**
>
> **For many are called, but few are chosen.**
>
> **Matthew 22:14**

David began to soul search, to determine if he was ready to receive the position of leadership. David knew that at one time, Saul had run well. But now he was witnessing the collapse of the ministry of Saul. David was witnessing the vulnerability of a king in office. He knew that the road which lay ahead of him would have to be travelled skillfully. It was not for a man to challenge the seat of power with pride and cockiness, but to acknowledge the Lord as the captain of the ship.

David realized that many individuals were called into the ministry. Yet many fell flat on their faces. There were untold numbers of judges who received the appointment to lead the nation of Israel, but were seduced into wayward living and failed to accomplish what God ordained for them.

God puts leaders through all kinds of tests. He takes them through the wilderness. He strips them of their pride. He makes them go through all kinds of things that they don't understand that causes them to question themselves. This is all in the making of a leader. God literally forms and shapes a leader. So when you say, "God, use me as one of your leaders," you must be very careful about what you say. It is like holding a spiritual .38 to your head. What you are really saying is, "Lord, test me. Try me. Chastise me. Purify me. Strip me. Take my pride. Remove my ego, and so on." When God starts doing it, we start screaming, crying and saying, "God, leave me alone! What are You doing to me? Why don't You bless me?" Then God has to withdraw from that prayer and say that you did not mean what you said. Then you wonder why the prayer was not answered. It is all part of the package in the making of a leader. This is what Moses went through. This is what Elijah went through, and this is what David went through. All the great men of the Bible went through this. And now it is your turn— hang on! We get mad and upset and kick against the pricks. We call God names. We call people names. We call churches names. We get stressed out. We cry. We go to counselors and the counselors don't even know what is going on. Nobody can seem to fix the fix right, and if they can fix it right, God fixes another fix until we go through the process. We cannot get out of it, no matter what we do.

CHAPTER III

UNRESOLVED OFFENSES:
THE OPEN DOOR TO A DIVISIVE SPIRIT

It would be useless to study the Absalom spirit or divisiveness without studying who is vulnerable to receive such an attack of the enemy. A divisive spirit must grab hold of individuals in order for it to be successful. Division only has its effect if more than one person is involved.

First of all, a major door of discontent or offense in an individual's heart must be open for this spirit to operate. This spirit seeks out those who carry unresolved offenses in their possession. They seek to amass a following of people who will support their own agenda, which is always contrary to the purposes and vision of those in leadership. This divisive spirit often leads its followers out of the church, ministry or vision; causing division and bringing great hurt to all involved.

> And it came to pass after this, that Absalom prepared him chariots and horses, and fifty men to run before him.
>
> And Absalom rose up early, and stood beside the way of the gate: and it was so, that when any man that had a controversy

came to the king for judgment, then Absalom called unto him, and said, Of what city art thou? And he said, Thy servant is of one of the tribes of Israel.

And Absalom said unto him, See, thy matters are good and right; but there is no man deputed of the king to hear thee.

Absalom said moreover, Oh that I were made judge in the land, that every man which hath any suit or cause might come unto me, and I would do him justice!

And it was so, that when any man came nigh to him to do him obeisance, he put forth his hand, and took him, and kissed him.

And on this manner did Absalom to all Israel that came to the king for judgment: so Absalom stole the hearts of the men of Israel.

II Samuel 15:1-6

Absalom was first inflicted with this great divisive spirit as a result of not discharging an unforgiving spirit that was resident within his heart. Absalom was angry with Amnon for raping his sister, Tamar. He had a right to be angry, but the Bible says "...Be ye angry and sin not..." Absalom was required by God to deal appropriately with his anger. Instead, Absalom allowed his anger to graduate to a full blown offense.

This unresolved issue opened the door for a divisive and disloyal spirit to enter into his heart. Offenses may be the strongest weapon the enemy uses to divide the Church. According to Jesus, we cannot live in this world without experiencing offense. Though we are promised that offenses will come, it is not the offense itself, but our reaction to it, that determines our future.

There are other doors that allow a divisive spirit to enter in:

1. *Those that have complaints or injustices to be registered.*

And it came to pass after this, that Absalom prepared him chariots and horses, and fifty men to run before him.

And Absalom rose up early, and stood beside the way of the gate: and it was so, that when any man that had a controversy came to the king for judgment, then Absalom called unto him, and said, Of what city art thou? And he said, Thy servant is of one of the tribes of Israel.

II Samuel 15:1-2

Many times, as we desire to tell others how we've been mistreated or abused, we ourselves become vulnerable to sympathetic ears and seeds of discord. The Bible says that Absalom would affix himself in a position to have access to those that wanted to render a complaint (valid or invalid). One Bible version says that the people came to file lawsuits. It is precisely at the time when we seek to attain a verdict of not "guilty" do we often become guilty of receiving divisive spirits against those who violated us or even against those in leadership in which we desire to form a sympathetic ear.

2. *Those of us who always like to be affirmed.*

Absalom told the people, "Your claims are valid; you are right, you deserve the best."

II Samuel 15:3 (NIV)

39

When we get into a position where we must always be right, or where we can't receive correction or discipline, we are in trouble. Many times when we see ourselves as always right, we open the gate of our heart to the destructive seeds of the evil one.

3. *Those of us that like to be accepted and/or flattered.*

"Also, whenever anyone approached him to bow down before him, Absalom would reach out his hand, take hold of him and kiss him."

II Samuel 15:5 (NIV)

Many times, the difference between a good day and a bad day in our lives hinges upon the issue of acceptance. Sometimes, we may secretly desire for someone to accept us, accept our ideas, accept our company or even affirm us as a person. This is okay, but when exercised in excess, that same desire can make us vulnerable to divisive spirits. We begin to ascribe such credibility to the person from whom we desire acceptance, that we let down our guard and indiscriminately allow any seeds to become planted in the soil of our hearts.

As dealt with earlier in this book, flattery is also very dangerous. Those of us that thrive on flattery often become victimized by divisive strategies.

Absalom would extend his hand to the people (reflective of acceptance) and proceed to take their hands and kiss them. In other words, he would accept them, comfort them, flatter them and sow seeds of division without contest into their hearts.

And on this manner did Absalom to all Israel that came to the king for judgment: so Absalom stole the hearts of the men of Israel.

II Samuel 15:6

The end result was a foregone conclusion. The men of Israel became divided and the Church of David received an immense attack of the enemy. We must guard ourselves against the onslaughts of the enemy in this area.

CHAPTER IV

THE WEAK VERSUS THE STRONG

For they that are such serve not our Lord Jesus Christ, but their own belly; and by good words and fair speeches deceive the hearts of the simple.

Romans 16:18

There is a difference between a weak person (the simple) and a strong person. The difference is that the weak person has not yet developed their walk by principles. They are still walking by emotions. They are still walking by feelings. They are still walking subject to winds that blow and questions that come. Once they become strong, they no longer live by emotions. They don't live by gossip. They don't live by every wind that blows by. They simply live by principles. Therefore, when evil reports come their way, if they live by principles, the first thing they are going to do is to say to themselves, "I am not going to make any judgment on this situation because I have only heard this part." The Bible says in the Book of Proverbs that if you make any conclusion based on parts, you are a fool.

A man that lives by principles isn't thrown the moment he hears gossip or an evil report. He immediately puts that in the category of what the Bible says: "I have only heard one side. I will not make any decision." A person that is strong does not judge until the whole matter is before him. Second, he does not entertain evil reports against leadership. The Bible protects the leadership of the church and it says that, unless there are two or three witnesses, you are not even to entertain the accusation. That is living by principles. Every so often, as a pastor, I get a call from a member of my fellowship bringing charges against another member. Regardless of how serious the charge is, the first thing I do is to ask them, "Do you have two or three witnesses to verify what you are saying?" If there are no witnesses, I have to obey the Scripture. I have to say, "I am sorry, but I cannot handle the charge unless there are witnesses to what you are saying." As far as I am concerned, that ends it. That is living by the principle of the Word.

That is not being naive. To obey God's Word is never being naive. These are safeguards that God has placed in His Word to assure that accusations against leadership are handled appropriately. Rest assured that when a leader is out of order, God will see to it that in the season and time of His judgment, the two or three witnesses will not be a problem to obtain.

When we are developed and become strong, the Word of God will hold us. We'll respect those in authority. Husbands and fathers will be respected. We will respect all authorities that God places in our lives. That is a principle with God. If we have anything that challenges us to act contrary to the Word of God, or if we see somebody in a sinful act, the only thing that guides and controls us is the

Word. We are not supposed to get on the phone and call the prayer warriors. The Bible says if you see a brother taken in a fault, you go alone and speak to the individual and if he will not hear you, you still are not supposed to come to leadership. You are supposed to take another couple of brothers to them and then, if the individual is not responsive to them, you can finally bring the matter to leadership. These are the principles of the Kingdom of God. These are laws to keep order in the house of God. Matthew 5:23 says that if you have any ought against your brother, don't bring your gift to God, but instead go and be reconciled with him. We must live by the principles if we are going to be a strong church. We cannot be blown about by every rumor that floats through the air. Satan has a bucket full of evil reports all the time, but we deal with them through the principle of the Word.

Finally, brethren, whatsoever things are true, whatsoever things *are* honest, whatsoever things *are* just, whatsoever things *are* pure, whatsoever things *are* lovely, whatsoever things *are* of good report; if *there be* any virtue, and if *there be* any praise, think on these things.

Philippians 4:8

A strong person is not out inspecting everybody and trying to find something wrong. A strong person does not blindly accept every rumor that accuses another brother or sister. He just doesn't live that way. He has his mind on what is good. He marks what is good and avoids what is evil. Our job as believers is not to let evil penetrate the fellowship of the house of God, neither let evil penetrate us as individuals.

Teaching us that, denying ungodliness and worldly lusts, we should live soberly, righteously, and godly, in this present world;

Looking for that blessed hope, and the glorious appearing of the great God and our Saviour Jesus Christ;

Titus 2:12-13

The strong are obedient to the Lord. They live a godly life. We are here to minister to the needs of our brothers and sisters. That is the heartbeat we hear. We are supposed to be interested and involved in what will increase the house of the Lord. We are supposed to be interested in what will minister to the needs of people and not crave the negative things we can dig out or find out about other people. We are here to lift and exhort, not gossip and murmur.

THE VINDICATION OF GOD

And the God of peace shall bruise Satan under your feet shortly. The grace of our Lord Jesus Christ *be* with you. Amen.

Romans 16:20

This is a strong promise for the believer who lets God fight His battles against divisive people. Remember the context in verse 20. Paul is dealing with divisiveness. He is dealing with people who are offending others, and who are causing them to stumble. He says here that "the God of peace shall bruise Satan under your feet shortly." The word "shortly" used here is a poor translation because it sounds like it infers "someday this will happen." The word "shortly" actually means "he will bruise Satan quickly and swiftly." In other words, God is interested in His house. He is interested in keeping the house of the Lord in order so that the life of Jesus can flow through the congregation of the Lord. So Paul says He will come swiftly to bruise Satan who has tried to bruise the Church and He will put the enemy under your feet.

THE WEAK VERSUS THE STRONG

All forms of Biblical corrections are administered for the purpose of redeeming the person. It is never meant to destroy the person. It is easy for somebody to take a Scripture like this and misinterpret it and say, "Avoid them," or "shun them." "Put on your righteous robe and go the other way." No! The intent is not that you are better than they! When aversion and marking are called for, it is not to destroy that person, but it is to bring him to his senses. It is to let him know that divisiveness cannot continue in the house of God without consequences. It is a form of tough love. At times, love is a strong action. Love says, "No! That will not be tolerated."

One of the reasons we have a breakdown in families is because everybody wants to whitewash their problems. You cannot whitewash problems. You have to deal with problems. Love will administer correction, and that is the evidence of love. "For whom the Lord loveth, He chasteneth." That is what the Bible says. So if chastening comes even through avoidance and marking, its purpose is to redeem the divisive person from the snakepit of their sin.

> It is reported commonly *that there is* fornication among you, and such fornication as is not so much as named among the Gentiles, that one should have his father's wife.
>
> And ye are puffed up, and have not rather mourned, that he that hath done this deed might be taken away from among you.
>
> For I verily, as absent in body, but present in spirit, have judged already, as though I were present, *concerning* him that hath so done this deed,
>
> In the name of our Lord Jesus Christ, when ye are gathered together, and my spirit, with the power of our Lord Jesus Christ,

To deliver such an one unto Satan for the destruction of the flesh, that the spirit may be saved in the day of the Lord Jesus.

I Corinthians 5:1-5

Here we have an example of a person who is living in incest. The people in the Church of Corinth knew about it, but they took it lightly and the incest went on without anyone correcting the situation or confronting the people. The Apostle Paul wrote under the anointing of the Holy Spirit, and adjured them by saying, "You turn them over to Satan for the destruction of the flesh that their soul may be saved in the day of judgment." That might sound harsh, but the purpose of such measures is redemptive. This is not a sentence to hell, but it is a form of discipline that will inflict pain, sorrow and difficulty in such a manner that they would repent and straighten up their lives. There is something about pain, sorrow and difficulty that will cause a person to cry out to God in ernest, and it will crack the wall of pride and deceit that keeps a person in rebellion and sin. The Church at Corinth did just as the Apostle Paul commanded them to do. They removed the man from the fellowship because he would not cease from his incest.

CHASTENING BRINGS REDEMPTION

But if any have caused grief, he hath not grieved me, but in part: that I may not overcharge you all.

Sufficient to such a man *is* this punishment, which *was inflicted* of many.

So that contrariwise ye *ought* rather to forgive *him,* and comfort *him,* lest perhaps such a one should be swallowed up with overmuch sorrow.

Wherefore I beseech you that ye would confirm *your* **love toward him.**

For to this end also did I write, that I might know the proof of you, whether ye be obedient in all things.

II Corinthians 2:5-9

Now if you look at the Scripture above, you will find that in these Scriptures, the Church again went to the extreme. First, they tolerated the sin and they did nothing about it. Then when Paul wrote, they kicked the man out because of his sin. When the man repented and came knocking at the door of the church, the church would not allow the man in. Then Paul had to write another letter to the church to let them know that they must not hold that man back and cause many sorrows to continue, but to bring him back into the fellowship. Again, we see that the whole purpose of all correction in the Bible is not for the destruction of a person or anyone, but it is to bring healing to them, and initiate a response that will bring them to a place where they will ask for forgiveness. That must be the bottom line of any activity of judgment in the house of God.

DIVISIVE OR JUST WEAK?

Let us look at the difference here between a truly divisive person and a person who possesses a weakness that needs to be borne and supported. The interesting thing is that the weak person may actually exhibit and operate in some of the same signs as a divisive person. They are judgmental, critical and legalistic just like the divisive person. Many mistakes have been made in this area because of improper discernment as to which category a person is in before a decision is made.

It can be catastrophic if a weak person is categorized or termed "divisive," and it can be even more devastating if the same discipline that applies to a divisive person is inflicted upon them. Many weak people have backslidden and left the Church because of this. The thing is, we must understand the differences since they have almost the same signs. We must know why the Bible admonishes us to bear them up, to help them and to minister to them. Then, on the other side of the spectrum, the Bible admonishes us to mark and avoid divisive people.

It is very simple really. There is a difference between a person that has poor judgment and a person that just lacks integrity. You can challenge an individual over a decision and you are right to do so at times. But if you walk up to an individual and tell them that they deliberately and maliciously intended to do what you claim they did, then it is a different ball game. It is a different problem. When you lose confidence in the integrity of a person, there is nothing to which to relate to. Once the bonds of integrity are broken, you can no longer get along with them. You don't trust them anymore. They maliciously stab you in the back. They will purposely talk about you, rip you up, tear you up and spit you out.

A weak person might do the same thing with poor judgment and make a lot of dumb statements about you and talk about you because of their immaturity and weakness. The difference is one is teachable and adjustable, while the other is not. One can be brought, led and supported until they grow out of that immature state of legalism, criticism and gossip. You can do this by love, because there is an integrity factor that is in place. A good example of the criteria that Paul presented as the qualification for leadership is in I

Timothy 3. The qualifications of leaders are that they must be blameless. It does not say that they must be faultless, but that they must be blameless. There is a difference between blameless and faultless.

There is no one that is without fault, but integrity has to be in place. If integrity is not in place, then we have some real problems. When ministerial integrity is broken down and when people in the pulpit are using or making merchandise out of the people of God for their own interest, then we have a problem with integrity. We are to mark them and to realize that person does not need any communication link except there is repentance. Now a person who is weak can have integrity, but make poor judgment calls.

THE EVIL REPORT

Divisive people always come with a evil report giving false or incomplete information. It is a distortion of the facts. It is given with the wrong motivation: to cause the hearer to come to an inaccurate conclusion. These individuals come with a wrong motive. They come with a hidden agenda. They come with information that is not complete, that is either partial or false. They have an intent behind the information that they are pumping into you, or that they want to pump into you, to cause you to come to an inaccurate conclusion.

Now let me say this, the weak here are ignorant of what is transpiring through their activity. The divisive person knows exactly what he is up to. Again, integrity is the question. The weak may come and make many mistakes and cause a lot of hurt, but they are ignorant that they are damaging people by doing this. They are ignorant that they are destroying the fellowship and the unity of the house of God. They are ignorant concerning the fact that they are separating friends. They are ignorant to the fact that the things they think are incorrect, that what they have not checked, is actually defiling and causing harm to people. But the divisive person knows exactly what he is doing. He knows that he is getting even, that he can hurt the Body, that he can hurt the fellowship, and that he can separate good friends. His motivation is not pure and his goal is to bring division in the house of the Lord. It is normally done many ways: by words, facial expressions, tone of voice, gestures and silences. You can communicate a lot through silence. Have you ever seen a person who has just been asked a question and instead of answering, they just roll their eyes and say nothing? You know immediately that their response is bad.

Avoid it, pass not by it, turn from it, and pass away.

Proverbs 4:14,15

The unsuspecting, the innocent, the newborn, the immature and the carnal just believe anything that comes by. They buy it. The prudent man looks into it.

A wicked doer giveth heed to false lips; *and* a liar giveth ear to a naughty tongue.

Proverbs 17:4

The Scripture here makes it more clear. It simply says that if you have an offense or a grievance against someone, you are a prime subject to believe an evil report. Once a person is offended, it is amazing how easy it is for them to believe an evil report. All of a sudden, you start seeing things that are not actually there. You start misinterpreting and misconstruing things that really don't exist. Once you pick up an offense, it is an amazing thing how you can read into it. You'll see almost anything your little wild mind wants to see. All you'll be able to perceive is that they don't like you, or that they talked about you, and no one can tell you anything different. You've bought the lie, hook, line and sinker.

CHAPTER V

THE MARRIAGE OF
VISION AND THE HEART

In laying the foundation of the local church, the motives of those who serve in the inner circle must be discerned. Loyalty must be constantly evaluated. Although one may be gifted, being gifted in and of itself does not connote loyalty. The problem is that the seed of disloyalty can germinate and destroy the foundation of that gift. Disloyalty does not just make a sudden appearance. It develops in stages. If not discerned in its early stages, it can ultimately cause division in the work force of the local church.

Obedience is not submission. Many times people think that because they are obedient in doing a thing that they are submissive. You can have a person who is obedient and yet unsubmissive. We may perform everything that is expected of us, but if our heart is rebellious toward authority, we are not truly submitted.

Moreover thou shalt provide out of all the people able men, such as fear God, men of truth, hating covetousness; and place *such* **over them,** *to be* **rulers of thousands,** *and* **rulers of hundreds, rulers of fifties, and rulers of tens:**

Exodus 18:21

And I will come down and talk with thee there: and I will take of the spirit which *is* **upon thee, and will put** *it* **upon them; and they shall bear the burden of the people with thee, that thou bear** *it* **not thyself alone.**

And the LORD came down in a cloud, and spake unto him, and took of the spirit that *was* **upon him, and gave** *it* **unto the seventy elders: and it came to pass,** *that,* **when the spirit rested upon them, they prophesied, and did not cease.**

Numbers 11:17, 25

Moses picked men who feared God. Fearing God and proper living are closely related and are almost synonymous. These men were to have a healthy respect for God and maintain a holy life. Moses was to choose men of truth who consistently kept their promises, men of their word, men of integrity. He chose men who hated covetousness and who were not moved by financial gain. He looked for men who had the spirit of wisdom, for wisdom is needed in every area of leadership and in every area of life. They were to be men in their ministry. They were to have a reputation that was established and accepted by the people. God was very careful that Moses didn't pick a disloyal or divisive person.

BE LIKEMINDED

For I have no man likeminded, who will naturally care for your state.

Philippians 2:20

In the above Scripture, Paul refers to the leader he had raised up for the Ephesian church: "For I have no man likeminded as Timothy." Other translations say, "of equal soul" or "as interested as I am in the people of God." "For I have no one else of kindred spirit, no one like disposed." Now Paul was in prison. His ministry was limited, so he had to trust someone. He had to find someone that was able to carry on the ministry in his absence. He put his trust in his son in the faith, Timothy, because he was very loyal and not divisive. He was sure that Timothy would not split his church or ruin his ministry. He was sure that Timothy would not divide the people or sow any seed of discord in his absence.

Paul knew that no one except Timothy would handle problems, people and pressure the way he would handle them. Timothy was a man of proven character and ministry. He was one that was actually married to Paul's vision. Paul knew that Timothy was not and would not be concerned about his own. He knew that Timothy ate, drank and breathed the very vision that he had. He knew that Timothy was a true son in the gospel. Timothy had what Paul called a "kindred spirit." He was likeminded and equal in soul.

FINDING YOUR TRIBE

And there came of the children of Benjamin and Judah to the hold unto David.

And David went out to meet them, and answered and said unto them, If ye be come peaceably unto me to help me, mine heart shall be knit unto you: but if *ye be come* to betray me to mine enemies, seeing *there is* no wrong in mine hands, the God of our fathers look *thereon,* and rebuke *it.*

Then the spirit came upon Amasai, *who was* chief of the captains, *and he said,* Thine *are we,* David, and on thy side, thou son of Jesse: peace, peace *be* unto thee, and peace *be* to thine helpers; for thy God helpeth thee. Then David received them, and made them captains of the band.

For at *that* time day by day there came to David to help him, until *it was* a great host, like the host of God.

I Chronicles 12:16-18,22

Watch the same thing here. David was concerned about people that were married to his vision. He wanted people with the same DNA. He did not want to accept just anyone. It might sound stupid and crazy because at this time David just had a small church. You would think he would be happy for the crowd coming in to be a part of what he was doing. Instead, the opposite was the case. David looked at the future. He was concerned about divisive people and people who might sow seeds of discord, so he was willing to make sure that all who came to connect to his vision were properly filtered and tested to make sure they met the criteria. I believe that if it were to occur today, the leaders would be so glad for the crowd coming into the church, because they know the crowd will bring big offerings and that they will have the notoriety and popularity of having one of the largest churches in town. David was more concerned about building a strong local church that would serve the purpose of God for its generation.

David understood what most leaders today fail to understand. David was a generational builder. He was more concerned about the future than the present. He was more willing to risk anything to make his future ministry solid, than he was to embrace just anything. He wanted to build a solid foundation since he was just starting out. He wanted to filter the motives of those who were trying to connect with him. He wanted to make sure they did not have their own personal agenda. He wanted a group of people that would believe in his vision, understand where he was going, and that would believe in the gifting that God had placed within him. Even though he had one of the largest churches ever, he did not set out to build the largest church. That was not his original motive. His intention was to build God a people that would embrace what God had given him, no matter the number that became a part of the army. Because his motive was right, God blessed him immensely.

Let's look at how David filtered the motives of the people that came to him. The Bible says that when they came desiring membership in David's church, David went out to meet them and declared to them the real deal. You see, David was not concerned about membership. He was more concerned about those who would be PLANTED. We have Christians who have declared membership in twenty churches and are not a part of any. It is sickening. God only flourishes those who are planted. The Bible says that those that are planted in the house of the Lord shall flourish in the court of his God. David wanted to make sure that he was not just getting a bunch of flaky men who wanted to be a part of his work because of his notoriety or popularity.

DAVID TOOK A SECOND LOOK

David confronted them up front by desiring to know their motive. He wanted to know why they decided to choose his church. He wanted to know the motive behind their decision. He wanted to make sure that there was no personal aggrandizement behind their decision. He said, "If you come to me with clean motive, my heart shall be knit with your heart." This speaks of covenant. David wanted covenant conscious people. He wanted people who knew how to keep covenant and who would not break rank when things were hot and tough. Covenant people don't sow seeds of discord. Covenant conscious people don't split churches. Covenant conscious people are not divisive. They are people who are truly married to the vision of the house and to the vision of their leader. This was what David was looking for.

Leaders, hear me very carefully. Don't ever receive anyone into your chariot until you are quite sure that they are married to what God has called you into. Make sure that they are not with you to use your ministry as a springboard to something else. The Bible says that after their motives had been checked by David, he received them. Nobody knew how long it took David to check their motives. Sometimes it will take a while to actually discover the true intentions of people. Don't rush it. Don't just place people in positions. Take your time prayerfully in checking their motives. Step on their corns and bunions and see how they react. Request an early morning prayer and see how they respond. Do something to stir their nest that will reveal their intentions. Evil intentions cannot be kept hidden too long. They will be exposed after a while.

THE FILTERING PROCESS

And David longed, and said, Oh that one would give me drink of the water of the well of Bethlehem, that *is* at the gate!

And the three brake through the host of the Philistines, and drew water out of the well of Bethlehem, that *was* by the gate, and took *it,* and brought *it* to David: but David would not drink *of* it, but poured it out to the LORD,

And said, My God forbid it me, that I should do this thing: shall I drink the blood of these men that have put their lives in jeopardy? for with *the jeopardy of* their lives they brought it. Therefore he would not drink it. These things did these three mightiest.

I Chronicles 11:17-19

This is the aftermath of a tried intention. The Bible says that David just longed and wished that someone would give him a drink of the water of the well of Bethlehem. He was reminiscing about Bethlehem's well. Before he could complete his speech, three of the men who were with him broke through the host and risked their lives, just to get him some water from the well of Bethlehem. These three men were not stupid. They were men that were truly married to the vision of their leader. They were already knitted and planted. They didn't have their own agenda at stake. David's desire was their desire, and they were ready to die to fulfill his dreams. Even though David did not drink the water, their actions remain as a memorial attesting to the fact that David had reliable men who believed in what God had called him to do.

There are two major factors here that we are not seeing in the Church today, yet the Spirit of God is calling and crying for their manifestation in the Church. First, we are not seeing enough nobility in our leaders that they might say to their loyal servants, "I know that it cost you much to follow me and sacrifice this way." David would not use the water for himself only. Now watch this: David and his men poured out the water to worship God together. David did not pour it out alone. He included the people who were married to his vision in pouring the water out. It was a costly or priceless gift. And David knew that it belonged to God. And this is the kind of gift and offering that God receives.

God wants and expects us to give gifts and offerings that involve our lives. He wants us to give gifts that are connected to our lives, offerings that come from our hearts. He wants us to give something that is costly to us. That is what usually comes from men who are married to a vision. It was a gift that was connected to their lives.

Another element which we don't see today, that we must come back to, remains a glaring question that will prick each of our hearts: Why would these men risk their very lives, the lives of their families, their children and their jobs just to get water from the well of Bethlehem? The well of Bethlehem was a fortified well. The drinking well was the most heavily fortified position or place in the city, and David with all his men could not take the city. Knowing this, how on earth were these three captains able to go and fetch water out of it? What on earth can motivate a human being to risk his very life for another, forgetting his children and wife, just to fetch water for someone who was only reminiscing about wanting a drink? David had not even given them a military command to do so.

The only thing that can motivate men to risk their lives is a grateful heart of love that is married to the vision, ideas, and dreams of their leader. And the element that I see missing in the Kingdom of God today is that we have a lot of Christians who do not have a grateful heart of love for their fathers that have helped them, built them and turned them into what they are. I believe that the Christian leaders of today are not asking for your life. They are not asking for you to kill yourself. But they are simply asking: come to church, live in the Spirit, pay your tithes, give your offerings, stay committed to God, be married to the vision, bring your families to church, and do evangelism. Is this a problem to be compared to what happened with these three captains in the Old Testament? To some it is a problem because they have not learned to embrace what belongs to another man.

For at *that* time day by day there came to David to help him, until *it was* a great host, like the host of God.

I Chronicles 12:22

The Bible says that "day by day men from all walks of life came to David until there was a great army, an army of God." When you gather great men, you have the beginnings of a great church. Your men would have the ability to carry on the work of God in every department of the church just as you would; just as the Holy Spirit would anoint you and even better. Jesus prayed all night before choosing the twelve. When you gather men, you take a risk. Fervent prayer is the only wise approach.

THE DANGER OF NOT FILTERING MOTIVES

And when Paul had gathered a bundle of sticks, and laid *them* on the fire, there came a viper out of the heat, and fastened on his hand.

Acts 28:3

When you refuse or fail to filter the motives of people through the Word of God and through prayer, many times you will end up allowing disloyal and divisive people into your camp. This can be very deadly because it produces impostors. Look at the above Scriptures: Paul gathered sticks to build a fire to warm himself. In the sticks that he gathered, there was a snake and as soon as the fire heated the snake, it slithered out and attached itself to Paul's hand. When we gather men, we take a chance that in the pile of sticks there may be one snake. That is why we must be very careful in gathering. We must prayerfully check motives. Don't just look at their talents and giftings. A man with only a good talent or gifting will destroy your church. Look for men with both talent and strong character.

> Then Nahash the Ammonite came up, and encamped against Jabeshgilead: and all the men of Jabesh said unto Nahash, Make a covenant with us, and we will serve thee.
>
> And Nahash the Ammonite answered them, On this *condition* will I make *a covenant* with you, that I may thrust out all your right eyes, and lay it *for* a reproach upon all Israel.
>
> And the elders of Jabesh said unto him, Give us seven days' respite, that we may send messengers unto all the coasts of Israel: and then, if *there be* no man to save us, we will come out to thee.
>
> I Samuel 11:1-3

That snake may have enough willpower to attach itself to your hand and poison you in the ministry. Paul shook off the snake and we can, too. However, many times, not everyone has been able to shake it off. In the Scripture above, the Bible says that we should learn to judge not by the natural eye or natural ears. We must pray all night, like Jesus, who prayed for discernment in choosing the right individuals. It is possible to have more sticks than snakes, although at times it seems like we have chosen more snakes than sticks.

> Only Luke is with me. Take Mark, and bring him with thee: for he is profitable to me for the ministry.
>
> II Timothy 4:11

Another danger of not filtering the motives of people is that you will find untested people around your vision. Mark failed the team in a time of crisis. He vacillated and turned back. He let Paul down. He revealed a character flaw. He was later restored to the leadership team after his character was developed. Leaders take this kind of risk in choosing men who are untested and unproven. We might be surprised. We might be disappointed. Never be so disappointed that you refuse to restore a person that is weak. Keep developing the weak ones, even when their flaws are glaring.

Luke, the beloved physician, and Demas, greet you.

Colossians 4:14

For Demas hath forsaken me, having loved this present world, and is departed unto Thessalonica; Crescens to Galatia, Titus unto Dalmatia.

II Timothy 4:10

Another danger that this produces is that you may find yourself embracing unstable and unfaithful people. Demas was a good example. He was, for a short time, changed by Paul's presence. He was magnetized by Paul's ministry, but as soon as he was away from that magnet, he went back to his own character and denied the way of Christ. Demas is the mark of a disciple whose wavering impulse caused him to surrender the passion of sacrifice and sink in the swirling waters of the world.

THE KIND OF MEN GOD IS CALLING FOR

And when Abram heard that his brother was taken captive, he armed his trained *servants*, born in his own house, three hundred and eighteen, and pursued *them* unto Dan.

Genesis 14:14

We need men who are birthed in the main elements of the local church vision, principles and philosophies. They need to be birthed into the vision of the house, the principles of the house, the philosophy of the house, the standards of the house, the doctrine of the house, the procedures of the house and the spirit of the house. In Genesis 14:14, we see that Abraham's servants, who became warriors, were trained in his own house.

THE BIRTHING OF LOYAL MEN

The birthing process for loyal men and women requires a spiritual identification with the local church. As the vision and principles of the local church are set forth, they must be assimilated into their spirits, and not just his or her mind. A spiritual illumination must take place, resulting in a teachable spirit and a changed person.

CHAPTER VI

THE PAIN OF DIVISION

For the hurt of the daughter of my people am I hurt; I am black; astonishment hath taken hold on me.

Is there no balm in Gilead; is there no physician there? why then is not the health of the daughter of my people recovered?

Jeremiah 8:21,22

Is there no balm in Gilead? For hurting, wounded individuals, this question has probably been asked, in some form or another, over a thousand times. Divisive and disloyal sowers of discord are individuals who have often been wounded through no fault of their own. The Body of Christ plays an integral role in the treatment of these wounds. We must allow the love and compassion of the very nature of God to flow like a river through us to wash away the pain of those who are hurting. Did you ever notice that even those individuals (not in the Body of Christ) who suffer from drug addictions, negative behavior patterns, and crime filled lives, are usually hurting people who never received the proper guidance in their life? They need someone to help them deal with the root of their problem so they can be freed. Likewise, most divisive and disloyal people began as sincere, wounded sheep. But thank God, there is a balm in Gilead! There is a place of healing, soothing lubrication in which those who are suffering can find comfort, relief and remedy for their pain, discomfort and dissatisfaction. There is the anesthetic tranquilizer of the Holy Spirit which brings composure, calmness, and control in Gilead; the place of testimony and memorial. So why is not the health of the daughter of God's people recovered? How do wounded people become divisive and disloyal? Let us take a look.

I remember a woman I once met during my early years in Christ, who for confidentiality's sake we will call Cynthia. Cynthia was a mentally ill out-patient, who came to the church seeking help for her illness. It is important that I explain the intensity of Cynthia's problem, in order for you to understand the point. Though Cynthia was functional, she suffered from paranoia, complexes, low self-esteem, self-hatred, extreme dissatisfaction, and bitterness. She also possessed a violent spirit which would rise up within her at any moment to attack a person. However, she always chose to attack the person when they were alone and seemingly defenseless. It is helpful that I explain further to you that Cynthia's problem stemmed from her childhood. She was abused and badly mistreated. These things brought on her mental illness, because she could not cope with the pain. So in the bitterness of her soul, she would seek out others to attack who were seemingly defenseless as well.

As abused people usually become abusers, so divisive, disloyal people create others of their own kind. The law of nature is that everything will produce after its own kind. This is what divisive people do. They want someone to feel what they feel, think like they think, and agree with their views. If they win you over, they will feel like they finally have someone on their side so they do not feel alone anymore.

When Cynthia would come to herself, she would be very sorry for her behavior, repent and seek the help of the church for deliverance. But one devastating thing happened, which caused Cynthia to grow worse never receiving her deliverance. Due to the extensive care and attention she needed, no one had enough patience and compassion for Cynthia to work with her until she was completely delivered. They gave up on her. People merely tolerated her existence. They would say, "You better be nice to Cynthia or she'll lie in wait for you and beat you up," or "I cannot deal with her; she is crazy!" They began to treat her as an outcast, adding to the wounds she already possessed. Oh, if people could have only understood that she was a wounded individual who was only acting out the bitterness of her soul!

Cynthia's problem is best described by this Scripture:

From the sole of the foot even unto the head there is no soundness in it; but wounds, and bruises, and putrefying sores: they have not been closed, neither bound up, neither mollified with ointment.

Isaiah 1:6

You see, Cynthia is the perfect example of a soul whose wounds were never bound. Hear me child of God; you must watch how you treat others. When you offend the least one, you have offended our Lord, and have caused a wound or reopened a prior one. If that wound is not bound with love, it will fester and turn into a putrefying sore. Cynthia could have been whole today if someone had only recognized the root problem and taken the time to bind up her wounds. Once Cynthia saw that no one would help her, she became grossly dissatisfied with her church body and began to go around telling others of her plight. She may have thought it was merely to gain justification, but the spirit of discord was now able to enter her heart, take root, grow and germinate other seeds. She was now a full grown "discord sower." As such, she began to plant seeds into as many as she possibly could. Cynthia's original complaints of mistreatment were valid, but since her wounds were untreated, they had become infected. Now that infection oozed out onto others, causing them to be infected, too. Have you ever seen an infected wound? It is not a pretty sight, is it? Now imagine what it must be like to bear a spiritual or emotional wound!

The reaction of divisive, disloyal people can be likened to the children of Israel when they became dissatisfied with Moses' leadership after hearing the negative report of those who were sent out to spy the Promised Land. Eventually, they expressed their dissatisfaction.

> **And all the children of Israel murmured against Moses and against Aaron: and the whole congregation said unto them, Would God that we had died in the land of Egypt! or would God we had died in this wilderness!**
>
> **And wherefore hath the LORD brought us unto this land, to fall by the sword, that our wives and our children should be a prey? were it not better for us to return into Egypt?**
>
> **And they said one to another, Let us make a captain, and let us return into Egypt.**
>
> **Then Moses and Aaron fell on their faces before all the assembly of the congregation of the children of Israel.**

And Joshua the son of Nun, and Caleb the son of Jephunneh, which were of them that searched the land, rent their clothes:

Numbers 14:2-6

When the spirits of divisiveness and disloyalty creep in, they first send their buddies "doubt" and "question." "Doubt" will cause a person not to believe that the instructions of their leadership come from God. As a result "Question" will cause a person to scrutinize everything they say, and every move they make with the intention of finding something to prove their suspicions are correct. Once they think they have found something concrete, they run with it. They'll spread their suspicions all over the church and create havoc within the Body of Christ. The children of Israel scrutinized Moses the same way. I can just imagine what must have been going through their minds as they came to the end of their long trek in the wilderness, hearing such a negative report. This was a dangerous point for them, because whenever the blessing is about to come forth, the adversary will try to get you to do everything possible to hinder your own blessing, and disillusion you.

So in crept Doubt and Question. I can hear them saying "Moses keeps telling us that God is going to bring us into the Promised Land, but we have been hearing that for years. All we do is circle around this mountain. We never make it in. Why should we believe him now? It has not happened in the last forty years, so how could it happen now? This man is crazy! Now he wants us to venture out into some foreign territory where giants live to risk our lives while he sits back and waits for a report. Was not the first venture enough to prove that this so-called "Promised Land" Moses speaks of is not true? We never should have left Egypt. Let's kill him and his faithful followers, and find us a leader to take us back."

So all the dissatisfied, disillusioned ones in whom the enemy had planted seeds, now discussed how they felt with other people who were also able to be persuaded to believe the lie. They came to an agreement and proceeded to stone Moses, Aaron, Caleb and Joshua. This was their so-called "confirmation." It was the very thing they had been suspicious of all along, and all because they were dissatisfied with their leadership, and listened to that negative report. They felt wounded during their wilderness experience, neither understanding Nor accepting the chastisement of the Lord. If only they would have had hearts of understanding and pure love toward God, they would have realized that what they went through in the wilderness was not a nightmare nor a punishment, but the working of the Lord to try (reveal) their hearts, and prepare them for their blessing. They were bitter against Moses, but ultimately against God.

This untreated wound was an injury to their feelings. It happens when you do not agree with the way God is taking you. If you do not keep your heart with all diligence, you will become bitter, dissatisfied, and angry with God and the leadership He has appointed to bring you into the Promise.

FESTERING WOUNDS

To further understand the effects of untreated wounds, let us take a closer look at natural wounds. While doing so, picture in your mind a soldier in battle who became wounded, who is taken off the field, and has no medical facilities available to treat his wound.

According to the American Heritage Dictionary a wound is:

> *1. An injury, especially* **one** *in which the skin or other external surface is torn, pierced, cut, or broken.*
> *2. An injury to the feelings.*
> *3. Physical or psychological damage by maltreatment.*
> *4. The visible result of an injury.*

So a wound consists of open, uncovered flesh that was never meant to be uncovered. It is the visible result of an injury. It is important to recognize that the wound gradually develops into an infected sore. First comes the wound, then comes the infection. However, a wound is not so bad until it becomes infected due to lack of treatment.

No wound starts out infected. Nearly everyone in their childhood days fell down and hurt themselves periodically. We would run to Mama or Papa crying, and usually after proper care, the wound would heal rather quickly. If not, then medical attention was given depending upon the intensity of the wound. The degree of the intensity of infection within the sore depends upon the initial impact which caused the wound, and the amount of neglect. In the fullness of time -- the time in which it takes that wound to become infected and develop into a putrefying sore, the person is now able to infect others. Some may take more time than others, but the longer it is left untreated, the greater the risk of infection and the greater the potential to infect others. The potential is so great that a person may need to be isolated for a period of intense treatment until the healing is completed. This is what we need to do today to remedy this problem in the Body of Christ. We must isolate ourselves in our secret prayer closet, and isolate ourselves into the hands of good, strong, sound leadership who will be able to nurture us until our internal wounds can no longer be seen on the outside, because they have been totally healed.

REACTIONS TO OUR WOUNDS

A seed takes time to grow into a mature, full grown tree. First it is a sapling. Then it develops into a solidly rooted tree. This seed of discord within Absalom developed into a full grown tree over a period of forty years. This signifies the fact that we must be sure to destroy every root of offense within us quickly. If not, one day when it is full grown, a tree of divisiveness and disloyalty will germinate, causing other seeds to be planted in the hearts of weak, deceitful individuals.

> **But Absalom sent spies throughout all the tribes of Israel, saying, As soon as ye hear the sound of the trumpet, then ye shall say, Absalom reigneth in Hebron.**
>
> **And with Absalom went two hundred men out of Jerusalem, that were called; and they went in their simplicity, and they knew not any thing.**
>
> **And Absalom sent for Ahithophel the Gilonite, David's counsellor, from his city, even from Giloh, while he offered sacrifices. And the conspiracy was strong; for the people increased continually with Absalom.**
>
> **II Samuel 15:10-12**

We see here that Absalom stole the hearts of the men of Israel, but not the hearts of all the men. Only those who were able to be deceived. The loyal ones, the remnant, remained with their true leader, King David.

REHOBOAM'S MISTAKE

In the book of I Kings, Chapter 12, we find a national revolt of the children of Israel against Rehoboam, the son of the late great King Solomon, because of untreated wounds.

And Rehoboam went to Shechem: for all Israel were come to Shechem to make him king.

And it came to pass, when Jeroboam the son of Nebat, who was yet in Egypt, heard of it, (for he was fled from the presence of king Solomon, and Jeroboam dwelt in Egypt;)

That they sent and called him. And Jeroboam and all the congregation of Israel came, and spake unto Rehoboam, saying,

Thy father made our yoke grievous: now therefore make thou the grievous service of thy father, and his heavy yoke which he put upon us, lighter, and we will serve thee.
And he said unto them, Depart yet for three days, then come again to me. And the people departed.

So Jeroboam and all the people came to Rehoboam the third day, as the king had appointed, saying, Come to me again the third day.

And the king answered the people roughly, and forsook the old men's counsel that they gave him;

And spake to them after the counsel of the young men, saying, My father made your yoke heavy, and I will add to your yoke: my father also chastised you with whips, but I will chastise you with scorpions.

Wherefore the king hearkened not unto the people; for the cause was from the LORD, that he might perform his saying, which the LORD spake by Ahijah the Shilonite unto Jeroboam the son of Nebat.

So when all Israel saw that the king hearkened not unto them, the people answered the king, saying, What portion have we in David? neither have we inheritance in the son of Jesse: to your tents, O Israel: now see to thine own house, David. So Israel departed unto their tents.

But as for the children of Israel which dwelt in the cities of Judah, Rehoboam reigned over them.

Then king Rehoboam sent Adoram, who was over the tribute; and all Israel stoned him with stones, that he died. Therefore king Rehoboam made speed to get him up to his chariot, to flee to Jerusalem.

So Israel rebelled against the house of David unto this day.

I Kings 12:1-5,12-19

Now King Solomon's kingdom was taken away from him, and given to Jeroboam, because he disobeyed the commandments of the Lord by allowing his heathen wives to sacrifice to idol gods.

And it came to pass at that time when Jeroboam went out of Jerusalem, that the prophet Ahijah the Shilonite found him in the way; and he had clad himself with a new garment; and they two were alone in the field:

And Ahijah caught the new garment that was on him, and rent it in twelve pieces:

And he said to Jeroboam, Take thee ten pieces: for thus saith the LORD, the God of Israel, Behold, I will rend the kingdom out of the hand of Solomon, and will give ten tribes to thee:

(But he shall have one tribe for my servant David's sake, and for Jerusalem's sake, the city which I have chosen out of all the tribes of Israel:)

Because that they have forsaken me, and have worshipped Ashtoreth the goddess of the Zidonians, Chemosh the god of the Moabites, and Milcom the god of the children of Ammon, and have not walked in my ways, to do that which is right in mine eyes, and to keep my statutes and my judgments, as did David his father.

Howbeit I will not take the whole kingdom out of his hand: but I will make him prince all the days of his life for David my servant's sake, whom I chose, because he kept my commandments and my statutes:

But I will take the kingdom out of his son's hand, and will give it unto thee, even ten tribes.

I Kings 11:29-35

Solomon then oppressed the Israelites by placing a hard taskmaster over them, who afflicted them with hard service and chastised them with whips. Just imagine an entire nation of people in slavery, hard bondage and afflictions. When the people saw that King Solomon died, they pleaded with his son and heir, Rehoboam, to lighten their burden. However King Rehoboam denied their request and vowed to increase their afflictions. So when King Rehoboam sent for his taskmaster to give him the new instructions, they revolted, stoned the taskmaster to death, and sent for Jeroboam to make him King in Rehoboam's stead. This a classic example of people who are fed up with being wounded. There comes a point when they say, "We are not taking any more of this," and they avenge themselves for their mistreatment.

It still happens in society today. The wife or child who has been abused and wounded for so long suddenly rises up, realizing that they do not have to take that kind of mistreatment any longer. They'll say, "Take that! This is for all the times you wounded me!" And they shoot or stab with the intent to kill, not caring about the legal consequences or who else might be hurt by their actions. They just want out. Reason flies out of the window. They are out of control. They have reached the end of their rope. They are as David and his men were when Absalom sought to overthrow David's kingdom.

> **For, said Hushai, thou knowest thy father and his men, that they be mighty men, and they be chafed in their minds, as a bear robbed of her whelps in the field: and thy father is a man of war, and will not lodge with the people.**
>
> **Behold, he is hid now in some pit, or in some other place: and it will come to pass, when some of them be overthrown at the first, that whosoever heareth it will say, There is a slaughter among the people that follow Absalom.**
>
> **And he also that is valiant, whose heart is as the heart of a lion, shall utterly melt: for all Israel knoweth that thy father is a mighty man, and they which be with him are valiant men.**
>
> **II Samuel 17:8-10**

The Amplified Bible describes their state of mind best:

> **For, said Hushai, (to Absalom) you know your father and his men, that they are mighty men, and they are embittered and enraged like a bear robbed of her whelps (children) in the field; and your father is a man of war, and will not lodge with the people.**
>
> **Behold, he is hid even now in some pit, or other place; and when some of hem are overthrown at the first, whoever hears it will say, There is a slaughter among the followers of Absalom.**

And even he who is brave, whose heart is as the heart of a lion, will utterly melt; for all Israel knows that your father is a mighty man, and they who are with him are brave men.

II Samuel 17:8-10

These people were chafed in their minds, embittered and enraged, like a wild bear whose babies have been stolen. And we wonder why people, even in our churches, suddenly "lose it." They may have been quiet, seemingly meek and humble pushovers, but one day they let you know they will not be pushed around any longer. Their explosion always takes the form of revenge against those who have hurt them. And they literally send people running for their lives to escape their wrath. There is an old proverb that says, "You can't push a cat into a corner. If you do, he will come out fighting with all fours." That's just what the children of Israel did. They came out fighting, causing even those whose hearts were brave as a lion to melt in fear.

For a brief speculation, I will state that there does come a time when we need to "Come out fighting." However, you must be sure to fight against the adversary of your soul, satan, who is the author of all confusion. There comes a time when we must no longer sit passively by, while the enemy wreaks havoc and devastation in our lives. You must rise up and declare, "This is not my portion!" Those of us in the Kingdom of Heaven have endured much violent assault, but if we desire to see change, we must seek for it with great zeal and intense exertion (Matthew 11:12 Amplified - Paraphrased).

For the kingdom of heaven suffereth violence, but the violent take it by force.

Matthew 11:12

David and his people wanted their kingdom back, so they sought for it with great zeal and intense exertion or energy. The Scripture says:

> **And David went up by the ascent of mount Olivet, and wept as he went up, and had his head covered, and he went barefoot: and all the people that was with him covered every man his head, and they went up, weeping as they went up.**
>
> **And one told David, saying, Ahithophel is among the conspirators with Absalom. And David said, O LORD, I pray thee, turn the counsel of Ahithophel into foolishness.**
>
> **II Samuel 15:30,31**

Though they were pushed into a corner, David and his men prayed and sought the mind of God, not reacting foolishly to the devices of the enemy. As a result, God turned the counsel of their enemy into foolishness. By the same token, if we will diligently pray, seek deliverance, seek to forgive and not hold grudges against those who have trespassed against us, seek the mind of God concerning any wounds in our lives, and refuse to allow iniquity to reside in our heart, God will hear our prayers, deliver us from our enemies, bind our wounds, and cause us to reside in Gilead -- the place of testimony and memorial.

UNTREATED WOUNDS

Untreated wounds weaken the emotional state of an individual. It opens the door to anger and resentment, which in turn cause a strong feeling of hatred, and constant sensitivity in the area of offense. In many cases it causes paranoia. It produces the feeling of the "Poor Me" syndrome which says, "No one likes me. Everyone is out to get me. No one understands me, and no one is on my side." Many times, as in the case of Absalom, it may cause a person to seek notoriety or fame that they might be publicly promoted or that their injustice will be recognized.

The end result of the untreated wound of a soldier is sure death, just like the movies we watch where the wounded soldier never gets medical attention and dies. Yet, child of God, you must realize your responsibility too.

Let us pause a moment for two self-reflections which are vitally important:

1.   Have you shot any bullets which have wounded any soldiers and caused divisiveness or disloyalty to be planted in their heart?

2.   Have the wounds from any bullets you may have experienced been bound up with the balm of God or have they developed into putrefying sores which infect others also?

It is essential to understand that both the person shooting the bullet and the one receiving the bullet are accountable before God, because the one receiving the bullet now has the potential to become a "loaded discord sower gun," too. Whichever of these two you may find yourself in, deliverance is nigh you. The prayers at the end of this book will help to complete your deliverance. Remember, in every war people shape the outcome. You can shape your outcome and have a happy ending. It is your choice. I pray you make the right decision.

James Baldwin once said, "I imagine one of the reasons people cling to their hates so stubbornly is because

they sense that once hate is gone, they will be forced to deal
with pain."

CHAPTER VII

ROUTE OF A POISONOUS SEED

And she answered him, Nay, my brother, do not force me; for no such thing ought to be done in Israel: do not thou this folly. And I, whither shall I cause my shame to go? and as for thee, thou shalt be as one of the fools in Israel. Now therefore, I pray thee, speak unto the king; for he will not withhold me from thee. Howbeit he would not hearken unto her voice: but, being stronger than she, forced her, and lay with her.

And Absalom her brother said unto her, Hath Amnon thy brother been with thee? but hold now thy peace, my sister: he is thy brother; regard not this thing. So Tamar remained desolate in her brother Absalom's house. But when king David heard of all these things, he was very wroth. And Absalom spake unto his brother Amnon neither good nor bad: for Absalom hated Amnon, because he had forced his sister Tamar.

II Samuel 13:12

Here we read in Scripture the historical account that leads up to Absalom, the son of King David, falling into a realm of unforgiveness. Even though Amnon was one hundred percent wrong for what he had done, Absalom (just like you and I) had a responsibility to handle it correctly. Instead of allowing God time to take care of this great injustice inflicted upon his sister Tamar, the Bible reads in verse 22 that Absalom "hated" Amnon. Absalom not only held onto the offense, apparently he held a grudge against Amnon for a long, extended period of time. Grudges love to be held onto, but are very destructive in the lives of those who hold onto them. (See my book "Cursing The Darkness").

And it came to pass after forty years, that Absalom said unto the king, I pray thee, let me go and pay my vow, which I have vowed unto the LORD, in Hebron.

II Samuel 15:7

Next we see the account is picked up two years later. The same incident, the same offense, the same infraction has been allowed to remain in the heart and mind of Absalom for two years. Like a small snowball rolling down the side of a snow-covered mountain, the feelings toward Amnon were accumulating momentum and strength. The size of this destructive seed was increasing in proportion to the time that was elapsing. Many of us are in the same predicament. We have an offense or offenses lodged right in the chamber of our heart and we allow it or them to stay there.

THE GROWTH OF THE SEED

What's even worse than allowing this illegal alien to remain as a squatter in the chambers of our heart is that we periodically feed it and allow it to grow. We feed these offenses by pondering the incident over and over. We rewind the altercation, then play it, rewind and play it again, and so on. On a bad day, we even press pause, so that we can see it for long periods of time. All the while, the embedded seed increases in size. Absalom was now guilty of not only possessing an unresolved offense, but because of the length of time elapsed, he was the proud owner of an evil desire to avenge Tamar's victimization. Absalom has now become guilty of hoarding the ungodly desire to kill Amnon as payback for what he had done.

Then after desire has conceived, it gives birth to sin; and sin, when it is full-grown, gives birth to death.

James 1:15 (NIV)

The author of the Book of James warns us that after one's evil desire is conceived and sown into the soil of one's heart, the irreversible, progressive downhill slide of the individual begins. After the desire takes root in the soil of one's heart, the next offspring is sin. And when this sin grows up to full maturity and has babies, its children are death. So as innocent as the initial evil desire may seem, or as important as holding those grudges may appear, remember that the grandchild of those innocent desires is death. This is the fatal web in which Absalom was caught.

First of all, he had a legitimate reason for being angry— his sister was violated. He became responsible for his actions when he first gave birth to the evil desire of paying Amnon back with his life. Absalom feasted on these thoughts for two solid years. This was enough time to give birth to a monster ready to erupt. The initial desire gave birth to sin (the plot to revenge) and ultimately gave birth to death (the death of his character; the death of his dreams and vision; death to everything that could have been— even Amnon).

And Jonadab, the son of Shimeah David's brother, answered and said, Let not my lord suppose that they have slain all the young men the king's sons; for Amnon only is dead: for by the

appointment of Absalom this hath been determined from the day that he forced his sister Tamar.

II Samuel 13:32

David's nephew, Jonadale, so plainly paints the end result that Absalom's sole intention for two years was to pay Amnon back for his inflicted injustice upon Tamar. Revenge is never sweet. It is deadly.

THE TRANSFORMATION OF THE SEED

James 1:15 shows us that the embracing of an evil thought gives life to death. In the life of Absalom, this destructive seed reached gigantic proportions. He had fed this seed for two years and it had now begun to dictate the lifestyle of its owner. The seed became too enormous for one person to handle anymore. Soon it would be time to plant portions of the original seed in the vineyards of other men and women.

Most of the time, these poisonous seeds manifest themselves in the form of a seed of discord. The initial unresolved offenses are never satisfied in just wrecking the life of one individual. Its mission, if possible, is to travel as far in one's lineage as it can. The aftermath of the offense tries to live forever in as many lives as possible.

The next goal of an unresolved offense is to transform a divisive seed. The offense becomes the fuel that propels the seed of discord. Because of the time involved and momentum that is supporting a seed of discord, by the time this seed manifests its ugly head, only drastic moves can be taken to extinguish the forest fire that has now been set ablaze. The seed of discord has velocity similar to a one-ton boulder that is racing down the side of a mountain. Only drastic measures taken can ensure one from the pitfalls of this deadly tool.

> **There are six things the LORD hates, seven that are detestable to him:**
>
> **haughty eyes, a lying tongue, hands that shed innocent blood,**
>
> **A heart that devises wicked schemes, feet that are quick to rush into evil**
>
> **A false witness who pours out lies, and a man who stirs up dissension among brothers.**
>
> **Proverbs 6:16-19 (NIV)**

The Lord knows about the destructive force of a seed of discord. He knows that the momentum behind a divisive seed could cause havoc in an entire nation. No wonder the Lord gives more attention to, and therefore hates to a greater measure, the stirring up of dissension among brethren -- seeds of discord.

> **And it came to pass after this, that Absalom prepared him chariots and horses, and fifty men to run before him.**
>
> **And Absalom rose up early, and stood beside the way of the gate: and it was so, that when any man that had a controversy came to the king for judgment, then Absalom called unto him, and said, Of what city art thou? And he said, Thy servant is of one of the tribes of Israel.**
>
> **And Absalom said unto him, See, thy matters are good and right; but there is no man deputed of the king to hear thee.**

Absalom said moreover, Oh that I were made judge in the land, that every man which hath any suit or cause might come unto me, and I would do him justice!

And it was so, that when any man came nigh to him to do him obeisance, he put forth his hand, and took him, and kissed him.

And on this manner did Absalom to all Israel that came to the king for judgment: so Absalom stole the hearts of the men of Israel.

And it came to pass after forty years, that Absalom said unto the king, I pray thee, let me go and pay my vow, which I have vowed unto the LORD, in Hebron.

II Samuel 15:1-7

The above Scriptures represent approximately six years after the incident with Amnon and Tamar. The original offense is so far grown that the only place for it now is to be transferred into the soil of other lives. This seed's roots had grown so deep and so large in the soil of Absalom's life that now it needed to be extended into other soil. Just like a house plant whose roots become too big and deep for the pot they rest in, the owner must re-pot the plant. This involves obtaining a larger pot and more new soil. Absalom's life was fully consumed by now with the effects of this seed.

The Scripture here records that Absalom would get up early and affix himself at the side of the road leading to the city gate. This was a crucial position in regard to the city. It is at a city's gate that the strength of that city can be fortified or weakened. Absalom stood right at the road leading to the gate and began to deposit portions of his ill-fated seeds into the soil of other men and women. He remained at this task for the span of forty years. Obviously, he weakened the city of David by contaminating the ears of many that went by. This is how the seeds of discord were transformed.

From this story we see prophetically that we must guard the road to the gates of our city. There are four main gates to our city -- the eyes, ears, heart and, mouth. We must maintain strength in our city by strengthening our eye, ear, heart and mouth gates.

CHAPTER VIII

"ANOTHER SPIRIT" - THE SPIRIT OF THE ENFORCER

And the LORD spake unto Moses, saying,

Send thou men, that they may search the land of Canaan,
which I give unto the children of Israel: of every tribe of their
fathers shall ye send a man, every one a ruler among them.
                                                    Numbers 13:1,2

Here in the Scriptures, we first of all see that
Moses received instructions directly from God. Those
specific instructions were for Moses to dispatch men into the
land of Canaan to scout the circumstances and situations that
existed there. The very next verse demonstrates the
compliance and ease in which Pastor Moses was able to hear
and carry out the instructions of the Lord.

And Moses by the commandment of the LORD sent them from
the wilderness of Paran: all those men were heads of the
children of Israel.
                                                    Numbers 13:3

The Bible says, "And Moses by the commandment of the Lord sent..." We need more of this type of compliance in the Body of Christ today. This demonstrates the purity in which leaders of God's people should operate when receiving instructions from God. We need leaders that can effectively hear the voice of God and in turn carry out precisely what has been ordered. The commandments of God need not to be altered by addition or subtraction when received. Verse 2 shows that God said it...and Moses did it! This is how it should always be.

> So they went up, and searched the land from the wilderness of Zin unto Rehob, as men come to Hamath.
>
> And they ascended by the south, and came unto Hebron; where Ahiman, Sheshai, and Talmai, the children of Anak, were. (Now Hebron was built seven years before Zoan in Egypt.)
>
> And they came unto the brook of Eshcol, and cut down from thence a branch with one cluster of grapes, and they bare it between two upon a staff; and they brought of the pomegranates, and of the figs.
>
> The place was called the brook Eshcol, because of the cluster of grapes which the children of Israel cut down from thence.
>
> And they returned from searching of the land after forty days.
>
> Numbers 13:21-25

Moses sent one representative from every tribe amounting to twelve men. Along with the deploying of the men, Moses instructed them to observe the possessions of the people and the possessions of the land. Along with these commandments, Moses further encouraged the men by saying

"Be ye of good courage." This encouragement was spoken from the depths of Moses' heart. This encouragement came from the location of the heart that only a pastor possesses. It is called the "Pastor's Heart." It was the same encouragement that all pastors give their sheep when setting out to accomplish some segment of the vision.

The Bible tells us that the 12 men set out to accomplish what their pastor requested of them. They sought for the description that would be sufficient for their leader.

And they returned from searching of the land after forty days.

Numbers 13:25

This Scripture lets us know that the men took forty days to assess the land and ultimately fulfill what their leader had requested.

BAD REPORT CARDS

And they went and came to Moses, and to Aaron, and to all the congregation of the children of Israel, unto the wilderness of Paran, to Kadesh; and brought back word unto them, and unto all the congregation, and showed them the fruit of the land.

And they told him, and said, We came unto the land whither thou sentest us, and surely it floweth with milk and honey; and this is the fruit of it.

Nevertheless the people be strong that dwell in the land, and the cities are walled, and very great: and moreover we saw the children of Anak there.

The Amalekites dwell in the land of the south: and the Hittites, and the Jebusites, and the Amorites, dwell in the mountains: and the Canaanites dwell by the sea, and by the coast of Jordan.

And Caleb stilled the people before Moses, and said, Let us go up at once, and possess it; for we are well able to overcome it.

But the men that went up with him said, We be not able to go up against the people; for they are stronger than we.

And they brought up an evil report of the land which they had searched unto the children of Israel, saying, The land, through which we have gone to search it, is a land that eateth up the inhabitants thereof; and all the people that we saw in it are men of a great stature.

And there we saw the giants, the sons of Anak, which come of the giants: and we were in our own sight as grasshoppers, and so we were in their sight.

Numbers 13:26-33

Now was the time for the men to return to their leader and submit their book reports on what they had discovered and noticed while visiting Canaan. They marched straight to the pastor and his assistant, eager to have their report read before the people. Verse 26 says that they even had items for "Show and Tell." One after another, their reports read..."Surely the land floweth with milk and honey..., but!" Surely the fruit is magnificent...but!" Pastor Moses paid attention while student after student came with a similar report. The reports all posed a threat to the integrity of the vision. They all looked negative.

And Caleb stilled the people before Moses, and said, Let us go up at once, and possess it; for we are well able to overcome it.

Numbers 13:30

This continued for the first ten out of the twelve men. Things must have looked grim for Moses, until one of his ace students showed up and addressed the rest of the class..."Shut up you guys! Let us do away with your opinions and go possess that which we are able to possess. For we are well able to accomplish the task." This student of Moses was Caleb.

A BAD REPORT TURNED EVIL

But the men that went up with him said, We be not able to go up against the people; for they are stronger than we.

And they brought up an evil report of the land which they had searched unto the children of Israel, saying, The land, through which we have gone to search it, is a land that eateth up the inhabitants thereof; and all the people that we saw in it are men of a great stature.

Numbers 13:31,32

And they brought up an evil report of the land which they had searched unto the children of Israel, saying, "The land, through which we have gone to search it, is a land that eateth up the inhabitants thereof; and all the people that we saw in it are men of a great stature."

The men began to dispute what Caleb had to say and stood for. They stood toe-to-toe against Caleb and said, "No! We are not able to accomplish the task!" They went further to say that even that which was to be accomplished would utterly destroy them.

DEVASTATION OF A CONTRARY SEED

That night all the people of the community raised their voices and wept aloud.

All the Israelites grumbled against Moses and Aaron, and the whole assembly said to them, "If only we had died in Egypt! Or in this desert!

Why is the LORD bringing us to this land only to let us fall by the sword? Our wives and children will be taken as plunder. Would not it be better for us to go back to Egypt?"

And they said to each other, "We should choose a leader and go back to Egypt."

Numbers 14:1-4 (NIV)

Following the release of the evil report among Pastor Moses' congregation, there was found great confusion among the people. The purpose of divisive seeds among local churches are always deemed to do one thing; divide the headship from the rest of the people. This is exactly what began to happen. Despite the resume that Moses carried before the people, despite the miracles God wrought through Moses, and without further detailed investigations about Canaan, the Israelites grumbled and quickly began to think about replacing Moses as their leader. This happens today in the church. Despite the many victories a leader may have accomplished, despite the miracles done through their hands, and despite the track record of delivering an accurate Word from God, as soon as there is a questionable time, you always find some "grumbling Israelites" ready to hold an election for a new leader. You also find people considering returning to the "Good ol' days" of past fellowship and ministries.

CONFIDENCE IN GOD

And Joshua the son of Nun, and Caleb the son of Jephunneh, which were of them that searched the land, rent their clothes:

And they spake unto all the company of the children of Israel, saying, The land, which we passed through to search it, is an exceeding good land.

If the LORD delight in us, then he will bring us into this land, and give it us; a land which floweth with milk and honey.

Only rebel not ye against the LORD, neither fear ye the people of the land; for they are bread for us: their defence is departed from them, and the LORD is with us: fear them not.

Numbers 14:6-9

In the midst of total chaos, the Bible alerts us that two individuals who walked with those who spied the land began to address the company of the children of Israel. They began to give another report about the same incident. They began to sound a different tune about what the new Promised Land had in store for them. They reported that there was an "exceeding good land" that was ahead of them. The difference in their report was that they furthered their report with the involvement of the Lord. They said, "Even though the land holds these benefits, IF the Lord delights in us, IF He is pleased with us, it is He that will give us the land -- case closed." They held such a confidence in God that the issue of the land's possession was only contingent upon one thing and one thing only -- the Lord's pleasure in His people.

Many of us right now are facing the possession of our prophetic promises. Like the children of Israel, the question is not what and how many "giants" are in the way, but how much confidence do we really have in the Promiser of the promises?

CALEB'S SPIRIT - THE SPIRIT OF THE ENFORCER

But all the congregation bade stone them with stones. And the glory of the LORD appeared in the tabernacle of the congregation before all the children of Israel.

Numbers 14:10

Unfortunately, the negative seeds of the evil report had already taken root in the soil of the people's hearts. The church of Moses now wanted to stone his spokesmen. They wanted to silence the mouths of these that spoke as their leader. Often those that flow in the same vein or frequency as their leader— those that possess the spirit and heart of their leader— find themselves before the firing squad also when divisive seeds attempt to assassinate the leader.

Now the momentum of the evil report had increased to such a degree that it was out to mow down any adverse thing that would contradict its impetus. The people now wanted to eliminate their own— Joshua and Caleb. This is how deadly this spirit can be. Joshua and Caleb were two of their team members, but now they had come to an arena where even their very own were not worth saving. Entertaining the spirit of division is costly.

But as with any righteous deed, the Lord showed up on their behalf. The Lord went right to the leader as He always does, and began to list who was qualified and unqualified to enter into the promise.

Because all those men which have seen my glory, and my miracles, which I did in Egypt and in the wilderness, and have tempted me now these ten times, and have not hearkened to my voice;

Surely they shall not see the land which I sware unto their fathers, neither shall any of them that provoked me see it:

Numbers 14:22,23

The Lord told Moses, because these murmurers and complainers have witnessed God's mighty hand at work, seen His glory, His miracles and yet have not hearkened to His voice, they would be disqualified to enjoy the promise. Those that were unable to see the new land out of the eyesight of the Lord and those that planted the divisive seeds were being cut off from God's inheritance.

But my servant Caleb, because he had another spirit with him, and hath followed me fully, him will I bring into the land whereinto he went; and his seed shall possess it.

Numbers 14:24

But God was pleased with someone. He looked at Joshua and Caleb and commended them. He addressed Caleb as His servant and said that, because he possessed "another spirit" and followed Him fully, he and also his seed were eligible to possess the land. But what spirit did Caleb have that was so different than the rest? First of all, Caleb's spirit was in line with that of his leaders. He saw the situation through Moses' eyes. In fact, I believe this was actually a test to see who was cut out for the job ahead. Who had received the spirit of the leader? Caleb and Joshua. And we know that the baton was later handed to Joshua.

Caleb's different spirit allowed him to see negativity as something positive. The spirit within him came from a history of watching his leader receive commandments from the Lord and carry them out to the "t"! His spirit was shaped by his leader's track record, He watched God lead his leader, and his leader led him.

This spirit is greatly needed in the church today. The leaders of God's people in this hour should be birthing babies of Caleb all around them. After proven times of hearing God's Word and carrying out His ways, God's leaders should see followers begin not only to build a confidence in them as leaders, but also in the fact that they can and do hear the voice of God.

God also commended Caleb, because he followed Him fully. In other words, his growth and commitment was dual. Caleb had another spirit, because of his affiliation and trust in Moses, but he also had an unyielding faith in God. We must also back our confidence in the God of our leaders, because of the dual commitment. God said that the promise was available to such an individual as well as to their seed.

CHAPTER IX

ARE YOU INFECTED?

Let's look at some practical ways that would help to detect if you have been infected by a divisive evil report. You must remember that satan is doing everything to get you to stop growing, to pick up an offense, to get involved in divisive attitudes and to destroy your goods and purpose.

The first sign that you have been infected by a divisive spirit is when you believe something is true without hearing both sides. This is probably one of the major problems that we have in the church. It applies to leadership and to laity. We have Christians who are so quick to respond to reports without taking the time to hear both sides. This is so simple— you would think that we would be wise enough by now to realize you have to hear both sides before you can make a judgment call. I have had wives come to me and complain about their husbands: how their husband is treating them, how he doesn't give them sufficient money, how they feel like they are being controlled, and how the finances are being controlled by their husbands. While listening to them, I say to myself, "Let me out of here! Where is he? I am going to get this joker for you." So, I bring him in and I ask the man,

"Sir, I understand that you are having some problems in your home." And the husband says, "Yes, Pastor. I sure appreciate your letting me talk to you. We really had some problems." Then I say, "Tell me about it," and the husband says, "It's really been tough. I don't know how to control my wife's spending. We have already filed for bankruptcy once. She takes the money meant for groceries to buy herself clothes. She takes the credit cards, goes clothes shopping, and buys clothes for other people. I have sat her down and explained the problems she creates and incurs for the family. I finally had to take all the credit cards away from her, and accompany her to the grocery store to make sure she is spending the money for groceries." After hearing her husband, I said to myself, "She needs a good spanking!" But you know, this is really the way it is in life. If you try to make your decision based on one side, the Bible says you are a fool.

Another signal you've been infected is when you find yourself focusing on the negative aspect of the person involved. Statements like "Yeah, I never did like them too well," or "Yeah, they are kind of weird, aren't they?" or "Yeah, I just don't like the way they look at me." Your mind is ruminating on evil reports. Your focus is fastened upon the negative aspect of that person's life.

When you interpret a person's words and actions as supporting evidence to judge their motives, you can be sure that you are infected with a divisive spirit. Once you feel that a person is doing everything wrong, and you find yourself questioning and judging every minute detail of that person's life; their clothes, their laughter, their hair, their friends, etc., you will start seeing almost every thing they do as supporting the evil report that you have heard.

You've been infected if you find yourself backing away from the person in your spirit. After you hear about the evil report, you get an attitude toward that person. All of a sudden, you don't want to be around them, but you have not checked anything out about them or about the alleged accusations.

The next sign is talking to others about the evil report. Have you set yourself up as judge and jury and convicted the person already? Are you bitter toward them, even though they never directly offended you? Have you sided with their accuser, and picked up another man's offense? Your best friend or girlfriend may come and complain about a brother or sister with whom they have a misunderstanding. Without you knowing what actually happened, and even if your friend was right or wrong, you suddenly pick up their offense and you find yourself not liking that person......not because they did anything to you directly, but because of an offense that you picked up from your friend.

This breeds a major problem: the person from whom you picked up the offense finally goes to the individual resolves their offense. It's over. They become buddies again and your friend never tells you that they resolved their offenses. Now, you may go on for years disliking the other individual for what he or she did to your friend, and you were not even involved. And guess what? Your spirit is suffering from an infection! Your friend was cured, but you're still ill!

If you believe your actions in telling others the evil report is accomplishing the will of God— actually thinking that you are taking care of them, that you are "getting even" with them, or that you are helping God to chasten them, I have news for you. You're infected! God says judgment and vengeance is His. God does not need any help in chastening His children. He knows how to do it Himself and He is very good at doing it. The problem is we have many Christians who want to play God. We cannot hurry God. While we are so eager to see judgment, God says, "I will do it at My set time."

CHAPTER X

DETECTING A DIVISIVE PERSON

We want to grow up in life. We have a great work ahead of us. We have tremendous opportunity in God. We don't want to be caught stumbling and stopping our growth and getting detoured. We want to be able to focus on destiny and to serve without any hindrances. That is why it is very important in this hour to know how to quickly discern and detect a divisive person around you and in your fellowship.

The first way to detect and discern a divisive person is that these individuals will test your spirit looking for a compatible spirit. Are you a gossiper? Are you a whisperer? Do you have a negative attitude? If you have these spirits and more, you become a target or a prey of a divisive person. Divisive people are looking for a compatible spirit. If you are a gossiper, a backbiter or someone who has a nasty attitude toward authority, they have found someone upon whom they can dump their garbage. That is why we cannot be a gossiper or whisperer. We cannot walk around looking for negative things. The Bible says that we are to be wise under that which is good. We are to mark what is good and to be simple concerning that which is evil. We are not interested in evil reports. We are interested in good reports.

Second, they will always drop a negative seed to check out your opinions. They start by saying, "Well, I have a little problem with so and so. What about you? What do you think about the way the pastor was preaching on Sunday? What do you think about the way they raise offerings in the church?" The purpose for this deceitful strategy is to find out your stand concerning the church or the leadership. If they find out that your stand is very firm, they end up not wanting to associate with you. But if for any reason they find a slight crack in your stand, it becomes very easy for them to impregnate you with their divisive ideas and with their offenses. Normally, the final outcome is that you end up picking up their spirit and acting like they want you to act. That is why a keen discernment is needed to spot a divisive person and immediately avoid them.

Another way of detecting divisive people is that they will normally ask for your counsel with flattering, smooth, and persuasive words. They will say words like, "You know, you are such a man of wisdom. I just want to share a concern with you." They pat you on the back, telling you that you are wise and intelligent, that you certainly have insight they don't have, and that they need your help concerning the issues that they have. This tactic has often paid off with divisive people because they come off as very smooth, genuine and innocent. But their motives are very destructive. Their purpose is to enroll another candidate in their roster. It is very important to be alert and to raise our antennae so that we might not become a victim of a divisive, disgruntled person. Many times, the simple and the immature are usually unaware of the slick devices used by the divisive person.

Fourth, they create curiosity. "Did you know ...? Have you heard...?" and you say, "No, I haven't heard." Then they say, "Well, then, I better not say anything." Then your curiosity is piqued and you want to know badly. They've baited you on their hook! You have just been caught by the bait of a divisive spirit! You have been caught with your own curiosity! It is amazing how evil reports, gossip and rumors travel faster than the truth.

Fifth, they will get you to admire them. They will claim to have information that no one else knows. They always want to give the impression they are in the inner circle and that nobody knows what they know. They will claim to have facts and figures. If you are one that is inquisitive and interested in digging out dirt, you will end up eating up the worms of their plan. They will provide you with lofty information that will give the impression they are close and related to the inner circle.

Sixth, they will invoke vivid details that are always convincing, often distorting parts of the truth, by adding untruth. Their tongues are so smooth and sharp. They are detectives of darkness. That person is divisive. Their intent is not pure. Their motive is to hurt. Their motive is to tear people down and to tear up the purposes and the work of God.

CHAPTER XI

GUARD YOUR EARS

Are you of the opinion that once an evil report is dumped on you, it is hard to clear out? God wants us to be strong and wise. God wants us to be able to discern right and wrong, good from evil.

When a person begins to tell you a divisive, evil report, and generally you can hear it coming, stop them immediately in their tracks and ask them this question: "What is your reason for telling me this?" You have a right to stop them. Don't be afraid of them. Ask them, "Are you widening or compounding the problem by telling me?" Ask them, "How am I going to help in this problem?"

Second, ask them these questions before they start dumping their garbage on you: "Where did you get your information?" If they refuse to tell you, it is a sign of an evil, divisive spirit. If they begin to say, "Well, I really can't tell you. It is private information." Then you must quickly realize that there is something wrong. Never be afraid to confront a divisive person. Be bold and don't be scared! If you don't confront them and their reports, they will continually come to you and use your ears as a garbage container. When you confront them strongly, they will make sure that the next time they come to tell you something, they will make sure they have their facts straight.

Third, ask them if they've gone to that person or to the persons directly involved. In other words, ask them if they have gone privately to the individuals involved and tried to resolve the conflict. You will find out that a divisive person will not go privately to resolve the conflict before coming to you. Why? Because the integrity is not there. A divisive person does not want a resolution. He wants to get even. He wants to hurt. He wants to destroy. He wants to annihilate somebody's reputation and this is the way he is going to do it.

Fourth, ask them if they have personally checked out the facts that are about to be passed on to you, or if they are just passing them on from some other rumor.

Fifth, ask them if you can quote them after you check it out. Ask them if they are willing to go with you to the person that they want to talk about. A divisive person usually will not do that. They will say, "No. It is hopeless. Nothing can really be done." Or they will insist on secrecy. The reason they say this is because they are afraid to face the reality that they are divisive. They will always say, "Don't quote me. I don't want any more problems."

Finally, take out a pen or pencil and a piece of paper and ask them if they are willing to sign their name to what they just told you. You will find out that a divisive person will outright refuse to do that. A divisive person will not be willing to sign anything because they have no integrity.

I believe that we are in for a surge of growth, and I believe that God is positioning us in this hour for a great harvest. Satan can never hurt us from the outside...... ever. But he can hurt us from the inside. If we are not wise and don't handle things right, satan can penetrate the house of God and bring division. We need to be very watchful and protect what God has given us.

CHAPTER XII

RESOLVING DIVISIVE CONFLICTS

And when Abram heard that his brother was taken captive, he armed his trained *servants,* born in his own house, three hundred and eighteen, and pursued *them* unto Dan.

Gen 14:14

Conflicts will always arise when there are a lot of people. It might be a result of a slight disparity, but the problem then arises when our conflicts cross the line and become contention. That is when it becomes divisive. Contention has to do with strife. Moses handled the hard cases. In the local church, conflicts are the hard cases. All churches, marriages, relationships and friendships in every part of the world experience the devastating effects of disagreement, discord and conflict. The early church in the New Testament encountered several such problems and survived. The main problem in most churches usually relates to an unresolved conflict that created divisiveness in the church.

God gave Moses the ability to handle the conflicts that arose in the nation of Israel. The set man or the leadership of the house today has the anointing of the Holy Spirit and the wisdom of God to handle various conflicts which surface in the church. An individual, a leader or a husband who does not know how to handle various conflicts will continually have little fires burning in his church. You don't resolve a conflict by getting a new suit, dress, car or position.

Conflict can make us hard or soft; bitter or better. It can make us lose confidence and become fearful to take the initiative when we see trouble because we are afraid of what might happen. Conflicts have great benefit when handled properly. It sounds silly, because we always think conflicts do not have any benefit, but that is not true. The first benefit of conflict is that it strengthens our character. The more conflict we have, the more we will pray, learn the Word of God and keep Him as the canopy over our lives.

Second, conflict makes us examine and purify our motives. Third, conflict reveals faults and flaws in us and in the church which otherwise would not have been revealed. Fourth, conflict teaches us spiritual endurance and spiritual carefulness. Fifth, sometimes it even jolts us into the will of God when we weren't intending it to jolt us anywhere. Not all conflict is negative. There are times when the Lord shakes the church and allows conflict to come so He can make needed changes.

WHAT IS CONFLICT?

Webster's dictionary defines "conflict" as "a striking together, a contest, to fight, contest, to clash, incompatibility, to be in opposition, sharp disagreement, emotional disturbance resulting from a clash." The Greek word "agon" was used to identify the place where the Greeks assembled for the Olympic games and watched the contest by the athletes. This word came to mean "struggle" or "combat." "Agon" is translated five different ways in the New Testament. It is translated in the New Testament as "conflict" in Philippians 1:30, as "contention" in I Thessalonians 2:2, as "fight" in I Timothy 6:12, as "race" in Hebrews 12:1 and as "agony" in Luke 22:44. There are dimensions of conflict that will possess all of these meanings, but wisdom will cause you to master conflict and receive all its benefits.

Conflict is a sister to contention. Conflict and contention need one another to grow. These two dwell and grow together whenever they are not handled properly. The word "contention" carries and implies the idea of quarreling, especially rivalry or wrangling, (as in the church at Corinth), or to have sharp feelings or emotions toward someone that affects our irritation level. Contention comes with the idea of strife or to be a lover of strife. It signifies the eagerness to contend.

HANDLING CONFLICTS

And certain men which came down from Judaea taught the brethren, *and said,* **Except ye be circumcised after the manner of Moses, ye cannot be saved.**

When therefore Paul and Barnabas had no small dissension and disputation with them, they determined that Paul and Barnabas, and certain other of them, should go up to Jerusalem unto the apostles and elders about this question.

And being brought on their way by the church, they passed through Phenice and Samaria, declaring the conversion of the Gentiles: and they caused great joy unto all the brethren.

And when they were come to Jerusalem, they were received of
the church, and *of* the apostles and elders, and they declared all
things that God had done with them.

But there rose up certain of the sect of the Pharisees which
believed, saying, That it was needful to circumcise them, and
to command *them* to keep the law of Moses.

And the apostles and elders came together for to consider of
this matter.

Acts 15:1-6

There are three important principles in handling
conflicts. In Acts 15, we see three basic principles which
were used by the leadership in handling conflict. First, we see
the principle of effective communication with an honest heart
and a teachable spirit. Second, we see the principle of the
leadership coming together to consider the matter before they
spoke to the congregation. Finally, we see the principle of
gathering all the facts from the parties involved. These three
principles will resolve any conflict in the local church.
Effective communication takes a lot of time and a lot of work.
Gathering facts can be tedious and painful, yet without all the
facts, you risk multiplying the conflict rather than solving it.

THE ATTITUDE OF A SERVANT

Jesus knowing that the Father had given all things into his
hands, and that he was come from God, and went to God;

He riseth from supper, and laid aside his garments; and took a
towel, and girded himself.

After that he poureth water into a basin, and began to wash the
disciples' feet, and to wipe *them* with the towel wherewith he
was girded.

Then cometh he to Simon Peter: and Peter saith unto him, Lord, dost thou wash my feet?

Jesus answered and said unto him, What I do thou knowest not now; but thou shalt know hereafter.

Peter saith unto him, Thou shalt never wash my feet. Jesus answered him, If I wash thee not, thou hast no part with me.

John 13:3-8

The foot washing service in John 13 provides insight into handling conflict. Three things happened in this chapter. First, Jesus laid aside His garments. The mature servant is willing to lay aside his reputation, position or status to deal with a problem. Many times we have to lay aside our titles and our positions to speak lovingly to one another and not to allow any of these things to intimidate people we deal with. A mature leader knows that in dealing with conflicts, he must expose himself and be deeply sincere and honest with people.

Second, Jesus girded Himself with a towel. This is a servant's dress. A true leader will gird himself with a servant's attitude. All leadership should be underneath pushing up. All leadership should take the servant's mentality, posture and attitude continually in every situation. Even when you are right and you have been accused of wrong, take the servant's attitude. Stoop and serve. When you are in a place where you can retaliate, take the servant's attitude. When you are in a place where you can bring vengeance on someone, remember the servant's towel. The robe of the servant is not the white collar or the title. It is the attitude of the servant that cloaks your heart.

Third, Jesus washed their feet. This was the function of a servant, showing Christ's humility and how unselfish He was concerning His own reputation. True humility expresses itself not in unfavorable comparisons of ourselves with others, but in wholehearted devotion to the interests of others. In I Peter 5:5, the Concordant Literal Translation says, "Tie on humility like a dress fastened with strings." Jesus showed the disciples how to minister one to another and how to prepare themselves for conflicts which would arise within the team and within the church. We can do this only when we wear the servant's towel.

Washing one another with a humble spirit and the power of the Holy Spirit becomes a key to relationships within the Body of Christ. Washing by the Holy Spirit is the evidence of maturity and the key to team success. We are responsible to lay aside our garments while washing. We are responsible to clothe ourselves with a servant's towel. Many conflicts will be washed from our hands and from the leadership team. The senior pastor must set the example of being a servant with a humble spirit, washing others and responding to those who come to wash him.

CHAPTER XIII

A PRAYER OF DELIVERANCE FOR YOU

I believe that you have been tremendously blessed by the Spirit of God through this timely book. Now that you have finished reading it and sense the very Spirit of God requiring a change of you, I urge you to join in praying this prayer of deliverance. And as you do, I want you to see the very Spirit of God destroying the yoke of bondage over your life.

Pray this prayer right now with me:

Father God, in the Name of Jesus, I thank You for opening my eyes to the truth. I thank you that the entrance of Your Word brings light, and I thank You that I don't have to walk in darkness any longer. I repent; I turn from my wicked ways, change my mind, and walk in Your direction. I recognize that I have been guilty of bringing division into Your Body. I have listened to things that I should not have listened to, and I have said things I should never have said. Lord, touch my tongue with the coals of Your altar, and burn away gossip and lies from my mouth. Father, I ask that you would purify my heart, and cleanse my motives. Lord, I ask you to help me guard the gates of my eyes, ears, and mouth that nothing which can contaminate my spirit will proceed out or enter in.

I ask for deliverance, for I determine in my heart to forgive and release every offense that I have taken against any individual. Teach me how to see as You see, and give me a new perspective so that I will not be trapped by a lie. Lord, purge me, and bring truth into my inward parts.

Father, I ask You to give me a teachable heart. Teach me how to accept correction without becoming bitter. Teach me how to submit to my authorities without harboring resentment. Lord, give me the grace to stay planted and bear the process of transformation without sowing discord, gossiping or taking offense. Let me hear Your voice in all things.

Heal my every wound, and cover me with Your balm. I thank you that by my firm decision to turn to You with all my heart, that Your grace is sufficient, and from this day forward, I will only do, say, and allow myself to hear that which edifies myself and the Body of Christ. In Jesus' Name!

Amen.

CHAPTER XIV

A PRAYER FOR A FRESH ANOINTING

Now that you have prayed the prayer of deliverance, I encourage you to recommit and rededicate your stand to that local church in which God has divinely planted you, by praying this prayer. And as you join in this prayer, I want you to believe that there is coming on you right now a fresh anointing that will make you faithful to the things of the Spirit.

Pray this prayer with me:

Lord, Jesus, as I have turned to You with all my heart, I thank You for Your forgiveness, for restoring me to right fellowship with You and my fellow brethren, and even for leaving me a blessing according to Your Word. I ask You, Lord, to guide me continually with Your eyes, that I may know how to wait continually in Your Presence, that I may to run without weariness, walk without fainting, and mount up with wings as an eagle, climbing from height to height, and from glory to glory according to Your will, plan, and purpose for my life. That I may be an instrument of Your glory, not one that will produce discord. I thank You for granting me a new walk with You as I re-commit, and rededicate my life, and the very intentions of my heart, to You. I pray that the words of my mouth and the meditation of my heart will be acceptable in Your sight.

I thank You for strengthening me with strength in my soul, for strength to win the battle. I thank you for giving me feet like hind's feet, and for warring hands and fighting fingers, that I may conquer every area of negativity. I thank You for new eyes, new ears, and a new heart that I might see, hear, know and understand Your voice and the move of Your Holy Spirit. That I might be a positively focused Christian. That I will not walk after the flesh, but after Your Holy Spirit in the Spirit of love, and unity. I thank You for a fresh anointing, and for increasing my ability to hear Your voice, and not the voice of the enemy.

Thank You for the continual ability to hear (even when You speak as you have spoken through this book) to reprove, correct, and instruct me in righteousness; for it is Your goodness that has led me to repentance that I might be restored to Your Kingdom. In Jesus' Name!

Amen.

To request a complete catalog featuring books, video and audio tapes by John Tetsola, or to contact him for speaking engagements, please write or call:

Ecclesia Word Ministries International
P.O. Box 743
Bronx, New York 10462

(718) 904-8530